# OTHER PEOPLE'S CHILDREN

# OTHER PEOPLE'S PEOPLE'S CHILDREN

Julia Wrigley

BasicBooks
*A Division of* HarperCollins*Publishers*

Copyright © 1995 by BasicBooks, A Division of HarperCollins
Publishers, Inc.

*Designed by Ellen Levine*

Library of Congress Cataloging-in-Publication Data
Wrigley, Julia, 1948–
    Other people's children : an intimate account of the dilemmas
facing middle-class parents and the women they hire to raise their
children / Julia Wrigley.
      p.  cm.
    Includes index.
    ISBN 0-465-05370-X
    1. Child care workers—United States—Interviews.   2.
Parents—United States—Interviews.   I. Title.
HQ778.63.W75   1995
362.7'12—dc20                       94-45703
                                       CIP

95 96 97 98 ❖/HC 9 8 7 6 5 4 3 2 1

*For the women, and men,*
*who look after other people's children,*
*and for my own daughter,*
*Elizabeth Wrigley-Field*

# Contents

# *Preface*

In a 1991 survey, over 40 percent of parents with family incomes over $75,000 reported they had hired caregivers to look after their children.[1] These well-to-do couples have the resources to get the kind of child care they want, and many choose care in their own homes.

This book examines private child care arrangements from the standpoints of both parents and employees. These relationships are interesting not only because they constitute a major form of child care for the increasing number of dual-career couples, but because they offer a window on social class differences in American society and what they mean for people's child-rearing strategies and values. Most parents in a position to employ nannies are well educated and hold high-status professional or managerial jobs. The women they hire to help raise their children can be worlds removed from them in background and education. This book asks how parents and caregivers deal with each other across this social gulf. It also looks at parents' strategies for securing the kind and quality of care they want from women who can be very different from themselves.

Caregiving relationships vary enormously from household to household, making care in the child's home "an unknown commodity of infinite variety."[2] Personality plays a large part in such relationships. Beyond this, employers vary in their level of wealth and in their ideologies regarding domestic help. Caregivers are even more diverse, with a small minority coming from middle-class backgrounds, such as college students who work temporarily as nannies, and others coming from conditions of hardship and poverty in developing countries. To capture this diversity and adequately study nannies required a large number of interviews in varied settings.

My research assistants and I conducted a total of 177 intensive, tape-recorded interviews, 76 with caregivers, 79 with parents, and 22 with the heads of domestic employment agencies.[3] Not surprisingly, most of the employers had young children, with just over three-quarters of those interviewed having at least one child under six. The employers' families had an average of two children. These employers had collectively engaged caregivers from twenty-nine different countries, including ten in Latin America, five in the Caribbean, eleven in Europe, and three in Asia.

The parents were highly educated; nearly all had college degrees and almost two-thirds had graduate or professional degrees. Occupationally, they were concentrated in the professions of medicine and law, in academia, and in business.[4] Most were dual-career couples, but we also interviewed many mothers who worked part-time or were not employed outside the home.[5]

The interviews usually lasted several hours. In some cases, parents and caregivers were interviewed several times, which allowed both a fuller exploration of their experiences and a chance to see how their situations changed over time. In twenty-one cases, we interviewed pairs of employers and employees, always separately, allowing us to see attitudes on both sides of a specific employment relationship.[6] All those interviewed were guaranteed confidentiality. No real names are used in this book and in a few cases identifying details have been changed.

The parent and caregiver interviews formed the core of the study, but we also interviewed heads of domestic employment agencies (and au pair agencies) to get a feel for the caregiving market as a whole. Its stratification shows up strikingly in the stratification of agencies. Some serve the most elite families of Beverly Hills and Park Avenue. They specialize in upscale nannies who boast some form of training, and who would not consider doing housework, while others serve families looking for a low-wage, all-purpose employee who may or may not speak English.

The interviews were conducted in two cities, Los Angeles and New York. They were chosen because both are ports of entry for immigrants and have large upper-middle-class populations, conditions that foster caregiving relationships. The cities have different immigrant streams, with Los Angeles having a very large population of workers from Mexico and Central America and New York having a more diverse immigrant mix. Census data show that in New York an extraordinary variety of women do domestic work.[7] When analyzed by place of birth, the largest group, about 14 percent, was born in New York State, but after that no state or country claims more than 7 percent of workers. In Los Angeles, of those domestic workers born in foreign countries, just over one-third come from El Salvador, a quarter are from Mexico, and one-fifth are from Guatemala.[8] More than three-quarters of the domestic workers in Los Angeles are not U.S. citizens, compared to just under half of those in New York.

To get diversity among employers, we selected them from two different neighborhoods in each city. In Los Angeles, the employers came from a middle-class area of Santa Monica (which is actually a separate city, but one entirely enclosed by Los Angeles) and from an upper-middle-class neighborhood, Westwood, just east of the UCLA campus. In addition, because the child care choices of highly educated, professionally employed women were of particular interest, in Los Angeles a "professional cluster" of women doctors, lawyers, and professors was interviewed.

The whole of the Los Angeles metropolitan area has a suburban quality, with heavy reliance on cars, but in New York it was important to find employers in both dense urban neighborhoods, where driving skills do not matter and where workers can arrive by subway, and in suburbs, where driving matters a lot and where employers tend to rely more on live-in workers. We interviewed employers on the Upper West Side of Manhattan, a middle-class, gentrified neighborhood where pre–World War II apartment buildings of sixteen or so stories mix with brownstones and occasional modern high-rises. We also interviewed employers in the suburban New Jersey town of Englewood, just across the George Washington Bridge from Manhattan but a world apart, with its spacious houses and tree-shaded streets.[9] Employers were found through neighborhood contacts, professional organizations of women lawyers and doctors, and referrals.

Finding caregivers to interview was more challenging. Many work illegally and are wary of strangers with tape recorders. They were located through immigrant social service agencies, neighborhood contacts, employers, and referrals from one to the next. Caregivers were also interviewed in parks. Particular attention was paid to interviewing caregivers of different nationalities and backgrounds. The sample consisted of forty-one Latina workers (interviewed in Spanish, with most from Mexico, El Salvador, and Guatemala), eleven Caribbean caregivers (from Jamaica, Grenada, Trinidad & Tobago, Guyana, and Barbados), two African-Americans, seven au pairs from Western Europe, and five each of Irish nannies, English nannies, and young women from the American Midwest.

The limits on caregivers' freedom became graphically evident during interviewing. Many live-in workers were not allowed to receive phone calls. Even when they said their employers did not mind their taking calls, it was seldom comfortable having the calls go through the employer. With live-in workers, even finding a place to hold the interview was a problem. Some caregivers were interviewed in cafés; others came to the interviewer's apartment. Latina workers did not suggest interviews in employers' houses, except when they were part of a pair. Other workers, more self-confident, asked employers' permission to have an interviewer come to the house. The most self-assured workers simply invited the interviewer to come, although they usually arranged interviews for when the employer was out.

Occasionally employers interrupted the interviews. During one session, a mother came into the room and started talking about what a considerate employer she was. The caregiver, with her back to her employer, rolled her eyes. The women had had a good relationship over eight years, but perhaps not quite as good as the mother thought. On another occasion, a Latina caregiver, interviewed with her employer's permission, had nonetheless expected the employer to be out of the house; instead, the employer was at home. At the end of the interview the caregiver whispered that her employer understood Spanish, so she had not felt able to talk freely. At a second interview, she discussed more openly her negative feelings toward one of the children in her charge.

I also met with caregivers informally when they picked children up from school, when they sat in parks, and when they talked together at children's gymnastics or dance classes. Occasionally caregivers arranged gatherings, where I could talk with several at once and listen to their own conversations. These occasions were always valuable, because they allowed a spontaneous quality that could be missing from interviews. Caregivers discussed things I would not have asked about, such as snooping through employers' papers. They also advised one another on how to deal with difficult employers and revealed their feelings about particular tasks employers wanted them to do.

Interviewing employers was much easier. Although busy, they had command of their own schedules and houses. Only one person contacted declined to be interviewed. Many parents seemed glad to have a chance to talk about issues they said they had often thought about privately, or discussed with friends, but had seldom had a chance to more systematically consider.

Many people helped with the research for this book. In Los Angeles, two UCLA graduate students, Benita Roth and Dolores Trevizo, did interviews and provided advice on the project as a whole. Their intelligence and insight added immeasurably to the project.[10] In New York, I was also lucky to have two good interviewers, Patricia Angarita, who interviewed Spanish-speaking caregivers, and Dalton Conley, who interviewed agency heads. Many people helped me transcribe interviews and I would like to thank them for their care with a laborious task: Patricia Angarita, Gloria Carol, Bernice Fischman, Manuel Guzman, Frances Kubica, Jack Levinson, Daniel Malpica, Jennifer Milici, and Erin Van Rheenen.

Raul Malmstein and Jean Kovath analyzed data from the 1991 National Household Education Survey on parents' use of caregivers, and Andrew Beveridge and Matthew Lindholm analyzed census data on caregivers' characteristics in New York and Los Angeles. I would also like to thank Judy Accurso, Bea Mandel, and Lynn Naliboff for helping me find employers to interview in three different neighborhoods.

Over the years, many friends and colleagues offered thoughts and suggestions on the study. Annette Lareau, who is also doing field research on families, has been an invaluable source of ideas, encouragement, and friendship. Colleagues at both UCLA and the CUNY Graduate Center have greatly stimulated my thinking on the issues explored in this book.

Hartry Field and Elizabeth Wrigley-Field put up with an interviewing schedule that occupied me for several years in two cities. They had to forgo family vacations for the project, which they did with good grace. My editor, Steve Fraser, helped by taking a broad view of the book's topic and by making excellent suggestions on how to organize the material.

The UCLA Academic Senate, the National Science Foundation/American Sociological Association small grants program, and the Professional Staff Congress–City University of New York research committee offered crucial financial support for the interviewing and transcribing.

Finally, I would like to thank the parents and caregivers who agreed to be interviewed. Their experiences and their thoughts and feelings about them were revealing and often moving. I appreciate the time and emotional energy they gave the project.

# CHAPTER 1

# The Parents' Dilemma

As more mothers go out to work, more couples are seeking child care. Many of those with the money to hire nannies consider this the ideal choice. They believe a nanny will give their children personal attention. They also think they can control the care their children get, as the nanny is their own employee. For parents of more than one child, a nanny can be cheaper than other forms of care. Working parents, who may be on the job long hours, value the flexibility of private caregivers who will stay late if need be and who will clean the house as well as look after the children. Nannies can ease parents' lives in a way that day care centers cannot. Seemingly, they offer a superior option for both parents and children.[1]

In the United States, day care centers, historically considered "something for poor, inadequate families," are still stigmatized.[2] Many parents think of day care centers as cold, unfeeling places where their children will not receive individual attention. In the 1980s, a rash of child abuse allegations against day care teachers intensified parents' worries about group care.[3] A Los Angeles mother summed up a typical set of reasons for hiring a nanny:

> I was scared about day care, there had been some horror
> stories, and I was frightened to do that, plus I really felt

that my son would get more attention being in the home. . . . My husband and I were both professionals, we had the money, and we really felt that we could hire the best and just make everything a lot easier for us.

These caregivers work in the privacy of their employers' homes and little is known about them. Most of the jobs are semi-underground, found through informal networks; many nannies do not pay taxes or have Social Security taxes paid for them. Immigrants represent a large part of the labor pool. Those in the country illegally face less risk of detection in private homes than they do in factories or hotels, and they are not barred by educational requirements.

This behind-the-scenes aspect of middle-class life acquired sudden visibility in January 1993 when incoming President Bill Clinton nominated Zoë Baird for attorney general. White House staffers expected Baird, the first woman ever chosen for the country's highest law enforcement job, to sail through Senate judiciary committee hearings. Instead, the hearings turned into a spectacle of attack and embarrassment. Baird, a highly successful corporate lawyer, and her husband, a Yale law professor, had hired an undocumented Peruvian couple to look after their three-year-old son. They had hired them knowing they were in the country illegally and they did not pay required taxes on them. First dismissed as "technical violations" by the White House, Baird's breach of tax and immigration laws elicited an outpouring of public indignation. After days of hammering by senators, Baird became the first Cabinet nominee to withdraw in 120 years.

The Baird debacle aroused public interest in the women who cared for the children of powerful dual-career couples. Reporters began asking who these women were, how much they earned, and how they were treated. A *Wall Street Journal* reporter wrote, "There is a dirty little secret in middle- and upper-middle-class America: Nannies are among the most exploited workers in the country."[4] Baird, of course, was hardly alone in neglecting to pay her employees' Social Security, disability, and unemployment taxes. Lawyer and former member of Congress James Corman said there was just one reason this abuse had long been ignored: "Crimes committed by well-off people against poor people do not get as much attention as crimes committed by poor people against well-off people."[5]

After the outcry over Baird's nomination, some parents changed their hiring practices. The IRS reported a 17 percent upsurge in first-quarter 1993 tax returns for domestic workers.[6] In Washington, a nervous Clinton administration forced a second attorney general nominee to withdraw because she also had hired an undocumented immigrant, even though the hiring was legal at the time and the nominee had paid all taxes.[7] The politically ambitious found they had a new and most unexpected area of vulnerability. Prominent figures in Washington began replacing their undocumented immigrant caregivers with women from the Midwest or European au pairs.[8]

"Nannygate," as it was inevitably dubbed, brought to light a form of child care hidden in private households. While nannies are a common sight in the parks of big cities, pushing children on swings and talking to one another, most of their work is performed out of view even of their employers. No government agencies regulate their labor or even count them. Parents learn through the grapevine about the ins and outs of the child care market, but their knowledge remains informal. The nannies themselves share tips on avoiding bad employers, getting raises, and dealing with conflicts, but they are not organized in any formal network.

## A COMPLEX RELATIONSHIP

In open-plan houses built for family togetherness rather than social exclusion, these parents share the care of their children and, sometimes, their living space with women very different from themselves. Race differences between parents and caregivers are immediately obvious, with dark-skinned women pushing blond babies in strollers a common sight in wealthy neighborhoods. Less visible, but just as pervasive, are class differences: middle-class employers hire working-class nannies.

People from very different backgrounds seldom have intimate encounters. Caregiving relationships, though, bring parents and caregivers together in the emotionally and culturally charged sphere of child rearing. Their conflicts, power struggles, and attachments illuminate tacit cultural assumptions. Only when people are faced with "the shock of the other" do they realize what their own values are. Many caregivers and parents have this experience daily. Based on 155 interviews with caregivers and parents in Los Angeles and New York, this book explores how parents and caregivers manage their differences. It examines middle-class parents' strategies for having their children socialized as they wish while being cared for by women who come from economic and social backgrounds vastly different from theirs.

The interviews show caregiving relationships to be enormously varied. Some employers and employees become personal friends. Others barely exchange a word. The most oppressed immigrant caregivers depict a world closer to Dickens than to Mary Poppins. One Salvadoran woman was slapped in the face by an enraged employer; another routinely had her purse searched the one day a week she left her employer's house. A Mexican caregiver did not know the name of the baby in her charge, after three weeks of working for her Los Angeles employers. Other parents and caregivers get along so well they partially fuse their lives. A Guatemalan caregiver, and eventually her husband and daughter, shared the home of a Los Angeles professor and her lawyer husband for seven years. Relationships differ as much in longevity as in closeness. One New York mother has employed the same caregiver for seventeen years. Another went through so many caregivers, she snapped their pictures so her young son could remember them.

Despite this range of experiences, there are constants in all caregiving relationships. The central dilemma for parents is that of incompatible desires. They would like caregivers who share their child-rearing values and who operate independently, but they also want inexpensive, reliable, controllable employees. Household employees substitute for parents, with the commitment and initiative this implies, yet they are intended to be subordinates. The "parent" versus "subordinate" balance varies among different caregivers and in some cases from time to time with one caregiver.

Parents who hire high-status employees are not always confident they can control them. They may hesitate to issue orders to an educated woman the way they would to a less-educated immigrant. The head of a Manhattan domestic employment agency said this was a factor in her failure to find a job for a twenty-seven-year-old American woman.

> It's hard for me to get her placed, because she's an American girl and fairly attractive. That keeps coming up. Like, "I don't know if I could tell her what to do" or "Is she too pretty? Ha, ha, ha." They make it a joke. Meanwhile, she's not getting hired. And she's the best. If someone's your equal, you can't say, "Clean the dishes, do the laundry." This is terrible to say, but perhaps they think these other women are beneath them.

Those parents who hire immigrants from Third World countries maximize class differences between themselves and their caregivers, but they also maximize the control they have. They can secure more housework from immigrant women than from caregivers who are more culturally similar to them. Experienced employers sometimes instruct new ones on the benefits of control. In one interview, a mother who is a computer consultant said she had complained to a friend that her Kenyan caregiver did not seem intelligent. The friend, an experienced employer, told her that sometimes it was better to accept "dumb" employees who were under the parents' control rather than deal with cocky ones.

Control of caregivers, though, can be hard to achieve. Parents can see whether the house is clean. They cannot see whether caregivers paid any attention to the children in their charge. When children are too young to talk, caregivers, who are, for the most part, unsupervised workers, can devote as much or as little energy to them as they please. An Irish nanny put it succinctly: "If you don't talk to the kid for two hours, who's going to know?" Because children's physical well-being is visible, many caregivers pay great attention to keeping the kids clean. Before parents come home, they scrub their charges and dress them in fresh clothes. The head of a domestic employment agency commented, "To me, that's the saddest thing in the world; it's almost like having to present the package intact at the end of the day. And maybe they're even restricting activity to achieve it."

Most middle-class parents have a high standard for the kind of interaction they want for their children. Some organize their entire child care search around finding it. Others may hope for it, but accept that they may not succeed in getting it; they try to compensate by providing engaged care themselves when they get home. Parents with these different expectations pursue quite different employment strategies, as the experiences of two dual-career couples in Los Angeles show.

## TWO APPROACHES

Mara and David Bensman, a doctor and an engineer, began by trying to hire a culturally similar worker when their first child was born. They were pleased to find an older Russian Jewish woman, because, Mara said, "We had stuff in common." The parents were part Russian. They soon learned cultural similarity brought no advantage, however. The nanny had strong opinions on baby care and argued with Mara about what to feed the baby. The Bensmans fired her and decided to hire from the abundant pool of Latina workers in the area.

At first, this choice seemed to work out. They found a Latina woman they liked, who stayed for two years but then left when she got pregnant. They renewed their search. Over the next five years, they had two more children and employed more than a dozen caregivers in succession. Most were Latina immigrants, but the Bensmans also tried hiring American women. Many blurred in Mara's mind. She could no longer remember their names or how she had found them. One stole from them and at least three left without notice.

The three American women the Bensmans tried introduced them to a new set of problems. When the Bensmans interviewed them, they came across as responsible and skilled, but each proved emotionally unstable. The first woman was "impulsive and unreliable." The second "was a loner, shy, awkward, and very inhibited, afraid to assert herself." The parents came home one day to find she had gone. She left a note giving her reasons. "One, that my husband walked around without his shirt, and she wasn't comfortable with that. And sometimes she could see the top of his underwear over his shorts, and that bothered her." The third American woman, a mother of eight from St. Louis, "was in the shouting therapy program. She would be gone for two nights a week for this therapy that involved shouting. And she started yelling a lot, reenacting her therapy, and that didn't work."

At the time Mara was interviewed, she had an Indonesian caregiver. This woman, though, was not the person Mara had actually hired. That woman, well educated, pleasant, and charming, accepted the job, but then did not show up, sending a friend in her place. Dismayed, the parents nevertheless tried to adapt. They checked the friend's references and decided to stick with her.

Mara attributed the rapid turnover to bad luck, although she acknowledged there might be problems with her interviewing technique. Mara's demands may also have been unrealistic.

She did not pay a high wage, but asked a lot of work: full cleaning and cooking, as well as looking after the three children. The caregivers' rate of departure makes it clear they thought they could do better elsewhere. The educated American workers Mara hired may have been downwardly mobile because of personal problems.

Mara had sought quality child care, but ended up with women who meant little to her children. Faced with a revolving door of caregivers, the children came to view them instrumentally, as people to get things for them and feed them. Mara and David tried to compensate by spending as much time as they could with the children in the evenings and on weekends. They read to them, did science experiments, and tried to create what Mara called an "enriched home." For Mara herself, the arrangement, while freeing her to pursue her career and lifting the burden of housework, caused more stress than she ever imagined when she first sought a caregiver.

Other employers more consistently strive to hire class or cultural peers. They want caregivers who share their child-rearing values. This can be particularly important to parents with professional jobs. They got their jobs through their educational credentials, and they usually hope their children will be able to do the same.[9] For these parents, a caregiver who keeps children safe, fed, and clean is not enough. Not even emotional warmth is enough.

A Los Angeles lawyer, Helen Dreier, married to a lawyer, considers only well-educated workers. This couple has four children: two teenagers from a previous marriage and younger children of six and two. In describing her hiring criteria, Helen said: "The basic idea was that I wanted someone whose value system and cultural system were not all that different from mine." Helen ruled out many people as unsuitable. She said that she did not want a "housekeeper-type person" taking care of her children, "someone who wasn't intellectually stimulating." She rejected American caregivers who struck her as having "hillbilly" characteristics.

This mother succeeded in finding the type of caregivers she wanted. These included a Brazilian woman with a master's degree whose husband was pursuing a Ph.D. "She was very instructive. Jill knew all her letters when she was eighteen months old." Helen also hired a self-confident young English woman, Emma; caregiver and mother sometimes clashed, because Emma had firm ideas of her own, but she was the kind of strong presence in Jill's life that her mother wanted. Helen's main complaint about Emma was that she did not truly appreciate her daughter's intelligence. "My daughter was an extremely precocious and headstrong child, and the weakness in Emma was that she could not appreciate my kid's real talents. Jill was extremely bright and extremely creative and Emma could sort of see that, but couldn't really appreciate it."

Helen left little to chance. Not only did she select caregivers carefully, she watched them for a day to make sure they were as good as she hoped. She also had her mother drop by unexpectedly and report to her on the caregivers' skills and behavior. Helen demonstrated how she wanted her children treated. "I try to be a role model for people who work for me. I will very consciously relate to my son in a way that I want [the caregiver] to relate to him when she's around." Helen reads many child-rearing books herself, picking up ideas, and she gives the caregivers books to read, with specific chapters marked. The Brazilian caregiver told Helen that she read more books for her than she had for her master's thesis.

Helen knew what she wanted and she never deviated from it. She consistently hired caregivers who had a professional orientation. She would never have considered the workers the Bensmans hired. With clearer ideas, and more money to implement them, she went for the top of the market. Those employers who exclusively seek class peers tend to believe, as Helen does, that their children are bright. Even more important, they think their children's natural intelligence has to be sparked and nurtured. They emphatically do not see child care as a job for the unskilled. They want their children exposed to ideas and engaged in creative play. Unlike the Bensmans, Helen and her husband did not think they had to compensate for their employees' weaknesses.


## RACIAL ATTITUDES

Not only social class and education count in determining caregivers' status; race does too. Historically, racial caste systems have funneled women of color into domestic work, whether they were African-Americans in the North or South, Mexican-Americans in the Southwest, or Japanese- and Chinese-Americans on the Pacific coast. As late as 1940, almost 60 percent of African-American women worked as domestics.[10]

Today, parents seeking caregivers seldom admit to racist attitudes, but owners of domestic employment agencies almost all say that significant numbers of parents refuse to accept black workers; if they do accept them, they expect to pay them less than white workers. One agency head in New York commented, "A lot of people will say, 'I will never hire a Caribbean woman.' And they say it on the phone. They don't know who I am or what I am." This agency owner added that Caribbean women have to be careful not to come across in interviews as being in any way aggressive. "If they're too boisterous, or if they are a bit pushy, they're not going to get a job." Raised in countries where racial lines are not so sharp, Caribbean women can be shocked to realize the extent of the racial stigma they face in the United States.[11]

Prejudice against black caregivers mainly affects Caribbean women, as very few African-American women now enter domestic work; most of those in the occupation are older women. Census data show that the average age of African-American domestic workers in New York City is forty-nine.[12] Agency heads say that almost none apply for jobs:

I never get any American black women. I once asked a
friend of mine who's black and she said that her mother did
that already. American black people have been slaves and
domestics for years. And after they scrub somebody's floor,
they get up saying "My child will never do this."

Parents' national and cultural prejudices can be remarkably
specific. One mother interviewed in Los Angeles said that she
would accept Salvadoran women, but not Guatemalans. A Los
Angeles lawyer refused to hire any Latinas. She would only
consider foreign-born caregivers who spoke English, but
because she thought they would inevitably lapse into their
native language while on the phone, she said the native language had to be one she liked. "I like French. I don't want
Spanish. It's not gonna be Castilian Spanish. Actually, I would
probably say that it's limited to French."

Although parents and caregivers create a private relationship, its terms are profoundly affected by the class and racial
inequalities of the larger society. Caregivers' status affects parents' ability to assign them tasks and control how they perform
them. Different parents strike different balances in their search
for employees who will both ease their housework burden and
provide what they consider good care for their children. The
caregiving market, informal and semi-underground, is highly
stratified, although specific educational credentials count for less
than a caregiver's ability to project herself as having middle-
class cultural resources. Parents evaluate this by the way she
speaks, dresses, carries herself, and talks to and about children.

## WHY IT WORKED IN THE PAST

Turning children over to servants is hardly new. The rich
have traditionally relied on servants for child rearing. In eigh-
teenth- and nineteenth-century England, for example, virtually

all upper-class parents hired nannies who took charge of young children. Nannies and children shared their own quarters, often a separate floor or wing of the house. Parents visited their children each day, but left details of their care to the trained people they hired.[13]

These families had to develop strategies for ensuring that their children absorbed the parents' culture and values even though they spent most of their time with servants. The task was made easier because children acquired their class positions by inheritance of land or titles. They did not have to learn complex intellectual skills. The main thing upper-class children had to learn was how to command respect from those below them and offer deference to those above them. Properly indoctrinated servants could teach the rituals of social behavior.

Parents kept children both socially and physically distant from servants, except those specially selected to care for them. In creating a hierarchy of employees, the parents made sure that those most like themselves were responsible in part for the cultural socialization of the child; at the bottom were those employees who dealt only with the most mundane physical care of the child and family.

Parents also often hired more culturally similar caregivers as the children got older.[14] For the youngest children, a nanny who could impart conventional social behavior might be all that was required, but older children moved from the realm of the nanny to that of the governess or tutor. Governesses were recruited largely from genteel but impoverished families. Governesses "*had* to be upper class, or at least genteel—which was why the financial collapse of a grand or well-bred house meant the surrounding families fell upon the unmarried and now impoverished daughters like flocks of ravening vultures."[15]

The differences between the family's world and the servants' world were not subtle; even young children could readily absorb them. And their parents reinforced the lessons of their daily experience by keeping an eye out for signs of their children becoming too attached to their caregivers. Such close attachments increased the risk that children would come to identify with the servants rather than with the parents who gave the orders. Parents could respond by firing nannies and governesses. Separating long-term nannies from their charges drove home the message that servants were not to be treated as full human beings.[16]

Upper-class children in the era of servants grew up in a social hierarchy where some people (including, someday, themselves) counted for a great deal, and others counted for little or nothing. They came to expect a strongly class-divided milieu, where there was constant daily contact between those who served and those who were served, but where this interaction was ritualized to emphasize the distinctions between the two.

## WHY IT IS HARDER TODAY

By the late eighteenth century, intellectually oriented parents in England's rising middle class were already attacking the use of servants to raise children.[17] They believed their children had to learn far more than rules of social etiquette; they wanted them to learn science, and modern languages, and skills of reasoning. They did not think servants had either the means or the motivation to foster children's curiosity and learning. Instead, critics of aristocratic notions of child rearing claimed that servants inevitably took a short-term view; they wanted children to be quiet and orderly, but did not care about their long-term development. Parents, these critics argued, needed to spend their own time with their children, both to win the children's love and to quicken their minds.[18] Two such writers, Richard Lovell Edgeworth and his daughter Maria Edgeworth, maintained that even very young children needed mental stimulation. They thought servants were completely unsuited for this task; they believed servants cared more about keeping children quiet and out of harm's way than about fostering their curiosity.

"A nurse's wish is to have as little trouble as possible with the child committed to her charge."[19]

Originally the province of a small intellectual elite, these ideas spread as the middle class grew and education became more critical for social advancement.[20] Not only did the supply of servants in any case begin to diminish, but domestic workers came to seem increasingly anachronistic. By the twentieth century, in both England and America, all except the very wealthy essentially raised their own children, and in most cases, mothers of young children stayed home to do so. They aimed to produce children who were not only healthy and happy but academically skilled.[21]

With access to good jobs now depending heavily on education, children today have more complex lessons to absorb than those in earlier societies did. Parents want even young children to develop their mental and social capacities.[22] Education-conscious parents encourage their young children to talk, they try to answer their questions, and they read to them. No longer is infancy considered a time when feeding and nap schedules matter more than intellectual stimulation. Child-development experts, and the mainly middle-class parents who read their books, consider this a vital learning period.

Emphasis on cognitive stimulation for young children accelerated in the mid-1960s.[23] This occurred in part because of the attention paid the federal Head Start preschool program; efforts to improve the performance of disadvantaged children had reverberations for middle-class children. Experts warned that parents had to pay close attention to their young children's development. The psychologist Burton L. White argues in his best-selling *The First Three Years of Life* that cognitive ground lost in the early years cannot be regained.[24] On a popular level, bookstores abound with titles such as *How to Raise a Brighter Child*. While critics bemoan these books and the "hurried child" they produce, the books continue to sell.[25]

Many parents with high-level jobs have acquired them on the basis of their own educational credentials. They would like their children to follow in their footsteps. Professional jobs are scarce, though, relative to the number of people who would like them. This increases parental anxieties about children's performance. The cultural critic Barbara Ehrenreich points out, "It is one thing to have children, and another thing . . . to have children who will be disciplined enough to devote the first twenty or thirty years of their lives to scaling the educational obstacles to a middle-class career."[26] Parents do not want their children to fall back, a threat families cannot dismiss.[27]

While there is much individual variation in child-rearing styles, there are also broad patterns related to social class. In general, middle-class parents are better able to prepare their children for school than working-class parents; their own class culture is akin to that of the school, giving their children a tremendous initial advantage.[28] In addition, as they themselves have high levels of education, they are in a position to actively transmit academic skills to their children. Middle-class children start school ahead of working-class children; they increase their advantage over the summer months, when schools are closed, suggesting their homes play an active educational role.[29] Despite the increased availability of schooling to all social classes in Europe and America since the Second World War, privileged families have not lost their academic primacy. These families know how to maintain their advantages, no matter what specific forms of schooling they encounter. In only two countries, Sweden and the Netherlands, has their advantage shrunk.[30]

Highly educated parents in professional or managerial jobs, whose own opportunity to be self-directed at work encourages them to value autonomy in their children, often create child-centered homes. These can be shocking to caregivers from other backgrounds.

Jeanine, a young African-American woman from a working-class background who was doing child care work for a few years as respite from high-pressure retail jobs, applied for a nanny position in the affluent New York suburb of Scarsdale. During a test day with the parents and their three children, Jeanine was appalled to observe an incident between a seven-year-old and his psychiatrist father. The boy got upset, screamed at the father, and threw all the towels in the bathroom to the floor. The father asked him to pick them up, but then, sitting with his wife and Jeanine later, he told her: "I'm very afraid that I was too harsh." The father said that he wished he had done more to find out why the boy was upset. Jeanine could not understand it:

> I'm listening and I'm going, Who is controlling this household? And I immediately wondered, Am I gonna control these kids or are they gonna control me? Because when I was growing up and *my* mother said, You do this, you did it like a half an hour ago. You didn't question it; you didn't scream and yell.

The employers had discussed a generous financial package, including paying college tuition if the caregiver stayed three years. Upon reflection, though, Jeanine did not think it was the family for her.

> Why do you have to sit here and rationalize with a seven-year-old about why he just threw towels on the floor? I just saw my future with this family. I thought, Oh my God, I know what is going to be happening. I'm going to be having these intellectual discussions with this seven-year-old. It doesn't make any sense.

Some caregivers come from cultures where adults do not think it necessary or desirable to encourage young children to talk or to develop individual tastes. Where poverty is widespread, adults concentrate on survival and have reason not to foster "high-demand" children. In these societies, "infant care is conceptualized as the provision of physical nurturance to ensure survival and growth." Adults hold and soothe infants, but spend little time talking with them. In education-oriented industrial societies, in contrast, mothers "engage the infant in

# CHAPTER 2

# Choosing Difference

Parents can create class and cultural chasms in their homes when they hire immigrant caregivers from developing countries. Parents and caregivers do not always share a language. Many parents turn these workers into low-skill laborers. They keep sensitive child-rearing tasks for themselves and delegate to employees the most routinized aspects of child care, including, particularly, the physical maintenance of young children.

Parents who routinize child care are minimizing expense and maximizing their control. Socially subordinate workers, many of them trying to support children or elderly parents, rarely reject tasks as beneath them. Employers can assign them housework and child care in whatever proportions they wish. The parents retain full control of child-rearing decisions. Not surprisingly, they pay an emotional price for these advantages. While some caregivers invest in their employers' children, no matter what their working conditions, many low-wage, revolving-door workers do not become close to the children in their charge.

Domestic work, despite being near the bottom of the occupational ladder, has its own limited career structure.[1] Workers can move from low-wage, confining, and demanding jobs to

ing, can often involve alienation. Some, though not all, caregivers are deeply socially subordinate; child care is embedded in a relationship of inequality. This can have costs for the women who do the work, and it can have implications for the care they can offer the children in their charge. Just as sociologists have found that the kind of work people do affects the behavior they encourage in their children, so too this can apply among caregivers. Those denied autonomy are unlikely to encourage it; those denied self-expression may not foster it among the children in their charge. This is not a commentary on the resourceful and courageous women who leave their homes, often alone, and begin lives in a new country or a new city; it is, though, a commentary on the employers' hope that quality care can thrive in difficult or isolating conditions.

The next chapter examines the experiences of employers and caregivers who have the greatest economic and cultural gulf between them, middle-class parents and immigrant women from developing countries.

These nannies would not even put a coffee cup in the dishwasher, her friends said, leaving the mothers with the housework. "I mean, it's unbelievable. I have doctor friends who still clean the toilets." Working twelve-hour days at a high-pressure job, she wanted an employee who would lighten her load, as well as look after her two school-age daughters.

After going through eleven employees in one year, the surgeon couple hired an experienced, capable Jamaican woman they consider close to ideal. She is well educated and interested in current affairs; the mother finds her good company. The caregiver accepts, though, that she will do the housework. Because these parents can afford top wages, they can hire someone to fill both caregiver and housekeeper roles.

## CONCLUSIONS

The practical dilemmas of caregiving relationships are matched by emotional dilemmas. Parents want contradictory things: They want caregivers to love their children, and yet can be disturbed if they love them too much.[33] Caregivers experience a more intractable dilemma than their employers: If they do not invest their emotions, their jobs can be alienating and unrewarding; if they do, they are deeply wounded when parents fire them or the children grow away from them. An agency head in Manhattan said years of experience had convinced her that caregiving relationships ran counter to human nature, requiring love as a job skill.

Caregivers help parents deal with the rigid demands of their own workplaces. They also help mothers deal with continued gender inequality in housework. Most important, parents who hire personal employees believe they have secured the best form of child care. Caregiving relationships may not, however, deliver on that promise. Interviews with caregivers and parents suggest these relationships, while sometimes positive and trust-

attentive and exciting communicative interaction (e.g., mock conversation) from the start, fostering the development of a more active and demanding child."[31] Middle-class American parents can themselves get worn down by their children's demands, but most hope, in hiring caregivers, that they have bought these adults' focused attention. There can, however, be culturally different interpretations of what kind of attention children require. These differences can form a backdrop to caregiving relationships. Some parents therefore seek caregivers they consider culturally similar to themselves, particularly once their children become verbal. It can help tip them away from "subordinate" caregivers or lead them to adopt a range of strategies to compensate for workers with a child-rearing style different from their own.

## THE CAREGIVER AS HOUSEKEEPER

Parents fit caregivers into an existing household division of labor, one that usually runs along gender lines.[32] Different types of caregivers do more, or less, of the work customarily assigned to mothers, as opposed to fathers. Despite several decades of feminist consciousness raising, women still perform more of the routine, repetitive tasks in homes than men do. These are the tasks socially subordinate caregivers (such as immigrant women from developing countries) are often assigned: the laundry, the bedmaking, the vacuuming, and, if they are live-in workers, the dinner cleanup. Higher-status caregivers disdain these tasks. Rather like the men in these households, they are quite selective about the chores they will accept without protest. Mothers with heavy work schedules thus have an incentive to hire class subordinates, rather than less cooperative class peers.

A New Jersey mother, a surgeon married to a surgeon, noted that although some of her friends, also highly paid doctors, hired English nannies, she did not want to go that route.

ones where they earn more and have some autonomy. The career structure is an uncertain one and no formal steps mark workers' progress along it. Workers cannot count on ground once gained being held; they can fall back in pay and working conditions. But overall, there are differences between the jobs obtained by newly arrived, inexperienced immigrants and those who are more acculturated. Immigrant women's employment traces an arc; employers can intersect this arc at many points, with some hiring workers who are at its lowest point and others hiring those from its highest.

This chapter looks at employers' reasons for hiring socially subordinate workers and at their strategies for dealing with them once hired. It asks, in particular, why some employers decide to hire the least acculturated, and most powerless, workers. From the caregivers' side, it asks what they think of their jobs and positions in American households and, for some, how they adapt to a kind of caregiving that can be drained of creative impulse.

## EMPLOYERS' STRATEGIES

Some employers focus on hiring cheap workers. This can lead to high turnover, but most accept this as a cost of their employment strategy. Parents have a variety of reasons for hiring workers who are at the bottom of the employment arc. In families where the mother does not work outside the home, she can supervise a caregiver; parents may not see a reason to pay high wages to an experienced or acculturated worker. Some parents of babies believe that infants do not require specialized care. And, finally, some parents would prefer an experienced, highly skilled caregiver, but do not think they can afford such a person, so they reluctantly "settle" for a new immigrant with fewer marketable skills.

Even some wealthy employers opt for a succession of low-wage employees. Karen exemplifies this type of employer. She does not work outside the home; she and her husband, a real estate developer, have four children, but they are widely spaced in age. The older two are in college, and the younger son and daughter are now twelve and eight. When the family moved to Westwood twelve years ago, they began hiring live-in workers (which they had done episodically before). Karen has now hired a long series of Central American women as live-in help:

> My feeling was that living in Los Angeles, there's this plethora of inexpensive and usually reliable people, at least as far as children are concerned. I hate to generalize by nationalities, but the Mexicans and a lot of the countries in South America, I think they're very family- and child-oriented . . . and I just felt comfortable with them and they were affordable.

Karen struggled to remember the names and nationalities of past caregivers. She has liked many of them, but has seen no reason to hold on to them for the long haul. Every year, before Karen and her children were to spend a month with her parents, "there would be a strong evaluation period as to whether it was worth keeping someone for a month and paying them, whether I really liked them that much. And usually it turned out that, for one reason or another, we didn't keep them."

Karen and her husband sometimes disagreed on whether a particular caregiver was good enough to retain. Her husband, she said, was not involved in hiring workers, but was often involved in firing them. One caregiver, "a woman with a certain class and dignity," became close to Karen's younger son, but Karen's husband insisted that she be fired because he did not think she cleaned the house well. In this family, the husband insisted his housekeeping standards be met, either by his wife or by the substitute whose wages he paid.

The caregivers were kept separate from the family; they ate by themselves and some wore uniforms. Not wanting to get embroiled in their lives and problems, Karen tried not to get to know them too well. She had thought about hiring an au pair, but thought an au pair would have taken up her time and would have injected her personality into the household. The Latina women Karen hired were expected to subdue their personalities. One Salvadoran did not, to Karen's displeasure. "You could never sit down and read the newspaper; she was always there, chatting away." Although an energetic worker, she did not survive the evaluation period.

Karen knew that she paid below-average wages. The highest wage she reported paying was $180 a week, while her neighbors, she said, often paid twice that. "I just knew I could get a competent person for a lot less." She deliberately hired workers who were recently arrived in the country and who spoke little or no English, because she thought they met her needs and were cheaper than more acculturated workers. Recognizing that her caregivers had lonely lives, she thought about introducing them to others in the neighborhood, but worried that they would then realize how much less they were getting paid. She compromised by introducing her employees to a caregiver across the street.

The caregivers, profoundly subordinate in the household, did not take on any complex tasks with the children. Karen herself spoke a simple form of Spanish, and she believed the caregivers found ways to communicate with the children despite the language barrier. She doubted, though, that the caregivers could think of activities to do with the children. Karen took the initiative: "When I would go out I would try to outline a program. I tried to give them enough activities to take care of the time when I was gone."

In this family, the mother relied on herself and local public and private schools to socialize her children into middle-class activities. She read to the children and carefully supervised their education. Karen did not believe caregivers had to contribute to this process; they lifted a great deal of labor from her, but only the lowest-level labor. Despite living in the employers' house, they had minimal connection with the family. No effort was

made to engage their interest or emotions in the work. Karen
had made one stab at hiring a more culturally similar employee,
and it had been a disaster:

> We had this really horrendous woman. I don't know what
> possessed me to hire her. She had been a teacher in Florida;
> she was older, about forty, and she was very severe-looking
> and sort of strange. I guess I thought I'd be getting someone
> who would be imparting knowledge to my children con-
> stantly.

She thankfully switched to hiring immigrant workers and never
reconsidered her decision. As a mother who was often at home,
she saw no reason to pay extra for skills she did not need from
workers or to hire people who would demand personal interaction from her.

Other employers hire newly arrived, low-wage workers
because they believe that infant care, in particular, does not
require any skill. A pair of Los Angeles doctors, the Lichtens,
fit this pattern, resisting employment agencies' pressure to offer
a higher wage to their eighteen-month-old daughter's live-in
caregiver.

> We pay $150 a week and they wanted us to pay a lot more.
> And I said that until the child was in more of a learning
> stage, in terms of teaching her things where I would actually
> demand more of a nanny type, that was pretty much our
> budget.

The Lichtens did not want a worker who would challenge
them. "We've interviewed a lot of people who were very sassy,
and we really don't want to be told how to bring up the child.
We want to be the ones giving the commands." But, despite the
low wage they offered, they wanted a caregiver who would
actively play with their child and be a stimulating presence. The
caregiver had to speak good English and had to accept sleeping

in the baby's room. Because the parents themselves worked long hours, the caregiver had to also; her duties included cleaning, cooking, and getting up with the baby in the morning. The Lichtens also specified that they did not want a caregiver with any relatives in Los Angeles, lest she be distracted from her employers' needs.

They liked their first caregiver, a Salvadoran, but she left after a year because she wanted live-out work so she could take English classes at night. The Lichtens respected her desire to improve her circumstances and skills, but did not modify the job they offered to try to attract other ambitious workers. They were unhappy with their next caregiver, a Mexican woman the mother described as "a disaster," who left without warning after two weeks. Their third caregiver, another Salvadoran, also left without notice less than a month after being hired. The Lichtens saw the women's departures as signs of moral failings: "When you're not dealing with an American or Western type person, the whole set of morals are really different." They tried again, hiring another Salvadoran.

After coming home from exhausting days, the Lichtens wanted a quick report from the caregiver, but no more. They had specified they wanted a quiet employee. "Because we interviewed people who I would have to instruct, in a nonoffensive way, 'Now, when I get home, you stay away.'" Since the caregiver does not have her own room, avoiding the parents in the evening requires finesse. After the baby goes to bed at 7:30 or 8:00, the caregiver has to make herself scarce. "She's usually either in the kitchen or the den, and we're in the opposite."

The mother tries to do things with the baby that the caregiver cannot do. She says she sometimes feels guilty about having the caregiver bathe the baby, even when she herself is home from work, "but I figure it's better for me to spend the time actually interacting with her on a more intellectual level." The parents have also enrolled their daughter in a preschool, where she will receive the attention of trained teachers, and they make sure both grandmothers stop by the house almost every day.

The Lichtens want someone who will be reliable and competent and who will demand very few of their resources, in terms of time, money, space, or interaction. They also want to be in charge of their own household. While their daughter is still young, they think low-wage immigrant workers are fine, but believe they may have to reassess this as she gets older.

Other employers hire recently arrived immigrant workers reluctantly, because they do not think they can afford a more acculturated worker. One such mother, Barbara, who is separated from her husband and lives in a modest apartment in Santa Monica, had a long succession of caregivers, most of whom left after only weeks or months. In one four-month period she went through ten caregivers. Barbara was trying to hire someone for $150 a week for six days of work. "There wasn't much available. I'm at the low end of the pay scale, so I can't really expect to get much." The women she did hire had little interest in her children. "The kids can tell, and they hated [the caregivers] and the kids were mean and they would scream at them and they wouldn't mind them. One of them even threw things at [the caregiver] and kicked her."

Given her children's poor relations with their parade of caregivers, Barbara was glad to enroll her children in preschool: "I wanted them to be around at least for six hours a day people who were professionally trained to bring up children. I didn't want my children to be brought up by a Mexican housekeeper without having some kind of influence that was from professional people." This mother had rejected the idea of an au pair, because she wanted cleaning and laundry done.

Parents with low-wage, unacculturated employees often do not have enough communication with them to gauge their actual feelings. Too suppressed and subordinate to speak their minds, most will quit before they will discuss any issues with their employers. AWOL workers are sending their employers a message, but it is not a message employers always choose to understand. Interviews show these workers can be deeply alienated, which is reflected in their high turnover rate; because the parents' employment strategies depend on a seemingly inexhaustible pool of immigrant workers, the parents usually accept turnover, even if it does not please them.

## WHY CAREGIVERS TAKE THE JOBS

Recently arrived immigrant women are in fact willing to take even jobs that strike the experienced as very undesirable. These women often must find work quickly. They do not have the financial reserves to adjust to their new environment before getting a job. They have to start earning and, in many cases, sending money back to their relatives in their home countries. Knowing little about the local labor market, and comparing their wages with what they would have earned at home, they can feel content with wages that later strike them as painfully low.

Immigrant women seeking first jobs usually look for live-in work. Most have divested themselves of dependents they must personally tend, though not those they must support: "Paradoxically, to be good mothers, women leave their children and migrate."[2] They recognize that if they move to the United States, they will not be able to get their own apartments for some time. They cannot afford rent and utilities. If they live with employers, they can save much of their pay. They also do not have to deal with transportation, a major problem in cities such as Los Angeles, where those without private cars can spend hours on buses every day.

Most of the immigrant women in our study reported that they came to the United States because they could not support themselves and other family members at home. Some suffered actual hunger in their home countries. Others came to escape violence in El Salvador or Guatemala. A few of the young single women said they came to the United States for "adventure," but most of those interviewed had dependents to support, either children or parents.

For those who left children, their sacrifice has meaning only if they can send money back. They are proud of supporting their children, although anguished by their separation from them.[3] A thirty-six-year-old Guatemalan woman, Carmen, who left three daughters, ages six, four, and two, said that she sends $300 a month home (out of monthly earnings of about $850) and that her daughters are "sad but happy because they now have some things." Mothers said that when they first separated from their children they felt intense grief; too busy during the day to dwell on it, they found nights the hardest. They reported crying themselves to sleep for months or even years after they first left their children. A woman from Guyana who left her son, now eleven, when he was six, occasionally talks to him on the telephone, but says it takes her two weeks to recover emotionally from each call.

New workers often take the first job offered. The luckiest ones receive assistance from friends or relatives already in the country, who orient them to the local job market and help them find good employers. A woman from Trinidad was able to live out from the beginning because a sister, also a caregiver in New York, helped her get a high-paying job. Those who find good employers are grateful. One woman from Guyana, who left children of two, three, and eight, said she could not have borne her pain except for her New Jersey employers' kindness.

Other caregivers, operating without assistance, or having aid only from workers who themselves are stuck in the low-wage part of the market, can end up earning almost nothing for long hours of work. A twenty-three-year-old Salvadoran woman who arrived in Los Angeles in 1987 looked after two preschool girls and was paid $85 a week at her first job, where she stayed for a year and a half; she worked from the time she got up at 6:00 A.M. until 11:00 at night. Another Salvadoran woman earned less than $100 a week for looking after five children. A Guatemalan woman worked six days a week, from 7:00 A.M. until 9:00 P.M., for $150 in 1988; it took her a year, she said, to realize that she had worse-than-average conditions: "I found out how the situation was over here in the United States. I found out that I had a job that was not paying enough and that I was being treated badly." Already unhappy, the woman left her job after being accused of theft, rejecting her employer's apology.

## ONE CAREGIVER'S EXPERIENCE

Newly arrived immigrants do often take low-wage jobs, but they can be dismayed by what those jobs entail. This was the experience of Beverly, an immigrant from Trinidad.

Beverly, a slender, pretty woman who projects dignity and friendliness, had moved to New York to earn money for herself and her eleven-year-old daughter, whom she left in her mother's care. One of eleven children, Beverly had little schooling. Within a week after arriving, she had landed her first job, obtained through an agency.

Beverly's employers had three boys, an eight-year-old and four-year-old twins, with a baby boy born shortly after she arrived. The mother worked part-time in an office, and the father had regular hours as an accountant. Beverly cleaned, cooked under the mother's direction, looked after the three older boys when they got home from school and preschool, and had primary responsibility for the baby.

The family lived in a large house, but Beverly did not have a room of her own. She slept on a fold-out couch in the den. The mother explained to Beverly that she did not like getting up in the night with the baby, because it left her too tired the next day. The baby slept in a crib in the parents' room, but when he woke up, the mother rang a bell to rouse Beverly, sleeping a floor below. As Beverly came up the stairs, the parents would pull down a screen in their room. Beverly would enter their room and try to comfort the baby. If she could do so in a few minutes, she would put the baby back in his crib. If she couldn't, she took him downstairs with her and put him in a crib next to her couch in the den. At 6 A.M., she would start getting the three older children ready for school. Beverly also looked after the baby in the early morning. The parents ate their own breakfast separately from the boys.

While the baby took his morning nap, Beverly cleaned. The mother often interrupted her work by peremptory commands to come and do something else. If the baby woke, the mother would cry "Beverly!" On the days when the mother was home, she often left the baby in Beverly's care while she read, talked on the phone, or wrote. Sometimes she played with the baby, but if he began to cry, she would immediately call for Beverly. This mother had divided baby care into desirable and undesirable parts. She played with a just-fed and happy baby, while Beverly dealt with the night wakings and the soothing of a cranky baby. In the common division of labor observed between mothers and fathers, this mother had managed to create something akin to the father's role for herself.[4]

The mother also assigned Beverly the routine care of her older children. Beverly ate dinner with the children, while the parents ate by themselves. After dinner, though, while Beverly cleaned up, the parents would spend time with their three older children and read to them.

Beverly liked the boys, particularly the eight-year-old, but never felt close to them. With no space of her own, with a day that stretched from early in the morning through the evening, she struggled just to keep going.[5] Beverly never saw friends in the evenings, but fell into bed as soon as she finished her tasks. She lost weight and felt exhausted and depressed.

After Beverly had worked there for some months, the father abruptly fired her, telling her that, although they found her pleasant, she was not strong enough to handle the three older boys. He told her to leave that day. The parents did not allow her to say good-bye to the boys, keeping them in an upstairs room while she left.

Beverly's employers had treated her as someone who could

lift tasks from the mother, but not as someone who could apply intelligence or insight to her job. They were not interested in acknowledging or developing her skills, and clearly saw their sons as receiving their socialization not from Beverly, but from the parents (in the evening time they spent together) and from their (private) schools. A neighbor told Beverly they had had many caregivers before her.

After losing her job, Beverly considered going back to Trinidad. She did not think she could endure another such experience. Her cousin persuaded her to try again, and Beverly soon found another job, this time in Manhattan rather than a suburb. Her new employer, who had interviewed eighty candidates, decided on Beverly when she walked in the door, impressed by her capable and pleasant air. Beverly looked after two preschool children in a more responsible position and developed a close relationship with the mother, who describes Beverly as a talented caregiver. Rather than confining her to drudge work, the mother organized her household so Beverly had the time and energy to actively engage with the children.

In Beverly's case, she advanced in the labor market not because of her own skill development, but because she happened to move from an employer who pursued a low-wage, low-skill strategy (where skills were not recognized even if present) to one who pursued a strategy of finding and paying for a worker able to take on the emotional and intellectual side of child care, as well as its routine aspects.


## WORK OVERLOAD

Most employers expect socially subordinate caregivers to do housework as well as child care. For many, this can lead to heavy workloads. This is especially the case for new immigrants.

Elena exemplifies a caregiver who found her employers'

demand that she simultaneously do housework and child care intolerable. Elena had finished high school in Guatemala and then had held a variety of jobs there, including office and factory positions, but not speaking English, and with no working papers, she found herself at the bottom of the caregiver market when she came to Los Angeles. She went to a domestic employment agency where she was placed in a room with other applicants. "We would have to sit there and wait for someone to arrive and check us all out as if we were Ms. Universe candidates. 'I like this one; I'll take her with me.'" Elena found this treatment painful, but insisted she was not embarrassed to be doing domestic work.[6]

Elena got a job working for a family with three children: two preschoolers and one seven-year-old. She found it difficult to vacuum and scrub while trying to keep an eye on her charges. Her divided attention helped precipitate a crisis in the home. The children had acquired a dog, which, in Elena's view, they tormented nonstop and turned savage. The family then installed a fence to keep the dog from the children, but one day the little girl let the dog out. The dog scratched the girl's hand and bit the leg of the middle boy, whom Elena described as "the terror." Elena was taking clothes out of the dryer when she heard screams. She ran outside, where an angry scene between the mother, the children, and Elena ensued. "In the mother's moment of hysteria she asked me why I wasn't watching them, why I wasn't checking up on them. So I asked her, 'Should I finish cleaning the house or should I attend to them?'"

In Elena's view, the mother was not really concerned about her children. "She was neither interested nor grateful about good care. All she wanted was to not have to deal with her children. It was that simple. She neither wanted to have to deal with them nor to know about them." For her part, Elena disliked the children, seeing them as rude. The mother, she said indignantly, would do nothing when her children insulted Elena.

Elena concluded that the only good thing about the job was that the mother paid her in cash. "If this is the way of all Americans, what a horror. What a horror." In Guatemala, she said, children did not express themselves so freely and were far more obedient.

Other caregivers with little power to limit or organize their tasks spoke of their frustration in trying to combine housework and child care. Carmen, a twenty-six-year-old Guatemalan with a fourth-grade education, took a harder line on the issue than Elena had. She eventually challenged her employer, a rare step for a newly arrived Central American immigrant. She rejected the employer's implicit definition of infant care as routine labor that could be done alongside other work.

Unlike many domestic workers in Los Angeles, Carmen had done domestic work in her home country as well. She had worked for four years, starting at age sixteen, taking of care of a doctor's children. This gave her a sense of how the job should be done and bolstered her in challenging her Los Angeles employer.

Carmen left her three daughters (ages six, four, and two) in Guatemala with her mother when she came to Los Angeles in 1989. She was separated from her husband, and felt getting a job in the United States offered her the best chance of supporting her children. In Los Angeles, she started as a housecleaner, because she thought her lack of English would matter less in that job than in child care. She ended up doing both child care and housecleaning, which made her very unhappy. "If I am rushing to do both, I will probably not clean well or take care of the children well. And in this country, the people, the employers, demand that you do both well." Carmen came into direct conflict with her employer on the issue:

> They required that I clean the entire house and the Señora wanted me to take care of the baby. The baby was very tiny, but was very accustomed to being held. So you had to hold her with one arm and clean with the other arm. That was impossible and one day I almost burnt her. Since then I have said no. Doing this work is going to get me in a serious

problem. So I told her that either I would clean or I would take care of the baby.

The employer responded angrily, arguing that the baby slept much of the time and weighed little. Carmen recalled that her previous employer in Guatemala had told her to make child care her priority, because otherwise there could be accidents. Despite her low level of education, Carmen felt a sense of professional standards, which her employer violated.

So I recalled everything that the woman from Guatemala had said to me. Now I told her, "I worked for a long time taking care of children. That is why I can tell you that I should either take care of the baby or clean." Well, she got so mad. She would walk around the house touching this and feeling that to see if I had cleaned it. She wasn't happy and she would tell me that my work was not good.

The situation came to a head when the employer refused to pay the agreed-upon wages, saying that the house was not sufficiently clean. Carmen did not argue, but left the job.

Other immigrant caregivers regretted that housecleaning duties conflicted with child care, but did not think that they could change the situation. A Guatemalan caregiver said of the girl in her charge: "I would sometimes feel sorry for the little girl because she would go to sleep by herself while sitting in a little corner. But I would say to myself that I didn't have time to sit down with her to hold her because I knew that they wanted the house clean."

Carmen finds her current employer much more pleasant, but she is still firmly wedged in the bottom of the market. Her new job also involves much labor for little money. Carmen sleeps in the baby's room, so she can handle nighttime wakings. The workday begins for her at 6:30 A.M., when the baby wakes, and lasts until 8:30 or even 10:00 at night, whenever she finishes the ironing.

The mother reserves some tasks for herself. She manages her six-year-old daughter's social life, taking her to friends' houses. The mother also does the shopping (a task very rarely delegated to a nonacculturated immigrant) and the cooking. But, to a degree unusual even for employers with live-in immigrant caregivers, the mother avoids tiring duties with her children. She takes the children to the park only when accompanied by caregivers. "She goes with us," Carmen said, "but it is up to me to play with the child. Sometimes she has someone else come with us so that I can be with one child and the other can be with the other child."

The parents also avoid the disorder of young children's meals. At first Carmen ate with the family, "but the baby would cause a lot of trouble, and one time when she was crying and crying, I took her to the living room with my food, so that she wouldn't cry. Then the Señora liked that, so we [Carmen and the baby] always eat in the living room now."

Despite Carmen's long hours, and extensive time with the baby, the mother, who is home all day, makes all the decisions regarding the children's activities and schedules. Carmen sees her lack of authority as a critical distinction between her experience as a mother herself and her experience as a caregiver.

> When you take care of someone else's children, you are under orders. If you need to call the [children's] attention to something, you can't, because you're just watching them. If they do something bad, you can't do anything unless they are in danger. With my own children, well, I am the mother, but with these children, I am just a babysitter. I am just here to watch them.

Carmen does not attempt to impose her own child-rearing values, seeing herself as "just a babysitter." Because the mother does not have a job and is home much of the day, she can play a managerial role in the household, directing lower-level help.

Carmen accepts her situation without complaint, appreciating the employer's friendly attitude toward her. She compares herself not with American workers, or with immigrants who have succeeded in getting higher wages, but with her neighbor. "Sometimes I feel I make very little when compared to what others make per week, but compared to my neighbor, I feel all right." Her neighbor is at the true bottom of the domestic worker market, employed not by wealthy Anglos but by another Latina, a domestic worker who is herself impoverished. The neighbor both cleans and takes care of the children, and earns $60 per week.

## CHILD CARE WITH LITTLE PLEASURE

Low-wage caregivers do not work in conditions that foster attachment. Many say they would rather clean houses than do child care. Housecleaners have the advantage of working for multiple employers, increasing their independence. They also have more control over their time than caregivers do, as they have to finish tasks rather than work for specified hours.[7] It is often hard for immigrant women to assemble full schedules of employers, though, and in some cities housecleaners need to be able to drive to get from job to job. This keeps some women in caregiving work, despite their distaste for it.[8]

Many live-in workers describe their unhappiness at being trapped in their employers' houses. Tila, a twenty-year-old Salvadoran, said she originally worked as a cashier. She compared child care work unfavorably to her previous experience: "The difference is that I had more fun at that job, more friends that are the same age. Whereas at this job I have to be locked up inside the house just cleaning and taking care of the baby. It's very different. And the fun is over."

Lourdes, another Salvadoran, also sees her job as boring and demanding. Her face reflects her hard life: she looks closer to forty than to her real age of twenty-two. The daughter of a janitor in El Salvador, she left school after fourth grade and began full-time work as a live-in domestic in Los Angeles at age fifteen (she lied about her age, claiming to be eighteen). Lourdes cares for a three-year-old boy, but dislikes the work. "To just clean or take care of children is really boring, but if we [Latinas] can't find anything else, we have to tolerate it because we need the money. I have to send money to my family on a monthly basis."

Lourdes does not express any affection for her charge. At first, she said, the boy didn't like her, but he got used to her. She thinks Anglo employers are overly fussy about their children. To her, the child's demands interrupt her housecleaning work. When asked her duties, she replied: "Everything! Everything! I clean, watch the children, cook, wash windows. Everything! Little by little, duties get added, whether it be after two weeks of being on the job or one month. They always add things. All of the jobs are the same."

## THE LANGUAGE BARRIER

Many newly arrived Latina immigrants face a particular difficulty in dealing with the children in their charge, an inability to speak English. In this, they are typical of other undocumented immigrants; one study of undocumented women immigrants from Mexico, carried out in Los Angeles in the early 1980s, found that nearly 80 percent spoke little or no English.[9] Some employers refuse to consider non-English-speaking workers, screening them on the phone for language ability. Almost 40 percent of the employers interviewed, though, had hired caregivers who spoke little or no English.

Some employers overcame initial doubts when they hired non-English-speaking caregivers, captivated by the appeal of particular candidates. A lawyer in Los Angeles, with a six-year-old son and a baby daughter, said: "I didn't want to hire a

Spanish-speaking housekeeper. I'm not fluent in Spanish. I thought that it would be no fun for my son. Then I thought, Well, I'll try it, because Rosario was so loving and nurturing and warm with the baby."

From employers' interviews, it is clear that many parents worry more about their ability to speak with caregivers than about their children's ability to do so. Parents who speak fluent Spanish (there were six such employers interviewed) are often happy to have Spanish-speaking caregivers. Other employers brushed up on high school Spanish, studied phrase books, or took Spanish classes. Some relied on Spanish-speaking colleagues at work to interpret for them if anything complex needed to be explained. There were, however, employers who spoke no Spanish at all, who had caregivers who spoke no English. They communicated through sign language.

Some employers prefer workers who do not speak English because they are cheaper than those who do. But many parents value their children's exposure to another language. They want their children to learn Spanish and see this as a positive aspect of having hired an immigrant caregiver. Unfortunately, in practice the children do not seem to learn much Spanish, unless the parents themselves also speak Spanish to them. Parents reported that few children became fluent in Spanish, no matter how much time they spent with Spanish-speaking caregivers. Even those children who came to understand Spanish often refused to speak it.

From the caregivers' side, not knowing the language of their employers can be frustrating. They worry that they will misunderstand employers' instructions or not be able to explain their own concerns. Afraid their employers will be irritated if they have to repeat things, they sometimes just nod when employers ask if they have understood. More seriously, not speaking English restricts the kinds of conversations caregivers can have with their charges. Researchers report that caregivers who speak often with children enhance their language development. Those who examine and talk about objects with children, or who describe activities, do the most to help foster children's language learning.[10] It is hard for caregivers who do not speak the child's language to play this kind of role; they do speak with their charges in Spanish, but the conversations tend to be fairly simple.

Perhaps because of the language barrier, many low-wage Latina caregivers approach their jobs anxiously. They describe themselves as oppressed by worry, finding the responsibility of keeping children safe to be overwhelming. A Salvadoran said the toddler she looked after was very active.

> He gets into everything. I have to be after him because in a moment of not paying attention he could fall, and Oh my God. When a child falls I feel very bad, because when their parents come and see a bruise I feel bad, bad, bad, bad, and I try at all costs to avoid such a thing.

Some are reluctant to take children out, fearing accidents. They also can worry about breaking things in their employers' homes or otherwise bringing their employers' wrath down upon them. With limited ability to communicate with their employers, they cannot easily explain any accidents or mishaps.[11] No Caribbean caregivers (or class peers) we interviewed expressed the same type of anxiety over possible accidents.

The most socially subordinate Latina caregivers describe their main task as "watching" the children in their charge. This "watching" does not necessarily entail any active engagement with the children. They speak less about the children's personalities than about any risks their behavior might present. Many describe their duties in very limited terms. When asked what her responsibilities were for the toddler in her charge, one Salvadoran caregiver replied: "Feed him. And change his diaper when it is dirty." Santos, a thirty-year-old Guatemalan caregiver with a sixth-grade education, saw her duties to her charges in much the same way: "Take care of them. Just make sure that nothing happens to them. That they don't go into the street. If I bring them to the park, to make sure they don't hurt themselves. When they're eating, make sure that they don't choke." The caregivers feel a commitment to the well-being of the children in their charge, worrying about them getting hurt, but some define that well-being narrowly.[12]

Apprehensive about employer displeasure, often unable to communicate anything very complicated to the children because of language differences, with limited educations, minimal autonomy, and heavy responsibilities, socially subordinate caregivers can find that their days pass slowly and their lives pass sadly. As Tila put it, too young to accept her fate, "the fun is over." It is not surprising that women who work sixty-hour weeks for sub-minimum-wage pay might not always bring a playful or inspired attitude to their caregiving duties, even though nearly all bring a strong sense of personal responsibility.

## A TEMPORARY JOB

In general, immigrant caregivers' hold on their jobs starts to weaken as soon as children become verbal. Many employers see immigrant women with little education as being suitable caregivers for young children, but not for older ones. Cultural differences loom larger for them when children are asking questions or learning language skills.[13]

No matter how attentive they have been, or how deeply attached to the children in their charge, the caregivers' utility to middle-class families diminishes as children get older. Many make a conscious effort to hold on to their jobs; they suppress their own values and they try to avoid challenging the children in their charge. One Guatemalan caregiver said that she took pains to always agree with her employer: "If she told me white was black, I would agree with her and say it was black."

Despite these efforts, few class subordinates can overcome the profound disadvantages of their social position. Middle-class parents increasingly move their children into their own cultural orbit as they get older.

Once-satisfactory caregivers can come to seem unsatisfactory under the new scrutiny. A New Jersey pediatrician, also married to a pediatrician, said that she and her husband began to notice that their Salvadoran caregiver provided little stimulation for their children: "And as the kids got older, it just got more difficult, and I wanted more out of somebody. She just wasn't that bright, but when they were babies, she was wonderful with my son, because he just really needed someone who carried him all day." A Los Angeles mother asked her Salvadoran caregiver to leave because she decided she did not want "custodial" care, but wanted someone who would be "enriching" for her children. She viewed her caregiver as having limited skills: "She was great at changing diapers, and, you know, kissing them and loving them. She was great for infants." But she lacked energy and had been, in the mother's words, "outgrown." Some parents we interviewed described their children as intellectually outstripping their caregivers. One mother said that her first caregiver had been adequate when her children were little: "Today this wouldn't work out, because intellectually, it just wouldn't be a satisfying enough arrangement, especially with Kevin, my six-and-a-half-year-old. He's smart as a whip."

Parents' changing attitudes as their children get older are reflected in their views on language issues. Some who thought Spanish-speaking caregivers were fine for their babies rethought the matter once their children became verbal. Seven of the thirty-one parents who hired non-English-speaking caregivers switched to English speakers. In some cases, this occurred because the children themselves became frustrated and said they wanted caregivers who spoke English. A Santa Monica mother described how her sons, ages four and two, became

increasingly resistant to their Guatemalan caregiver's speaking
Spanish to them:

> There was a point where they just decided they weren't
> going to speak Spanish. Maybe when [the older boy] went
> to preschool. And now they're incredibly anxious when we
> have somebody here who only speaks Spanish. They just get
> so frustrated and anxious that their needs aren't going to be
> understood and met.

The Los Angeles lawyer who overcame her doubts about hiring
a Spanish-speaking housekeeper changed her mind again when
her daughter started to speak. "I just decided that, seeing her as
a toddler, I wanted an English-speaking person again."

One Los Angeles mother employed a Salvadoran woman,
Adela, for about six years; despite occasional crises in their relationship, both women described it as close. Adela became so
attached to the two girls in her charge that her own daughter
felt bitterly jealous. Even Adela herself said that she had taken
better care of her employers' children than she had of her
daughter. Adela had no formal schooling at all (her father had
required her to work in the fields), but she had been able to
assume much responsibility for her employers' household. The
mother thought that Adela was outstanding when her daughters
were infants and toddlers, but she became more dubious once
they reached five or six. For babies, "any loving, kind, nurturing, intelligent, responsible" person would do; for older children, more was required.

> I love Adela with all my heart, but her idea of art is very dif-
> ferent from mine; Adela would not enjoy taking the kids to
> the art museum. I believe that what you put into their little
> heads in these formative years, five, six, seven, and eight, is
> crucial. Expose them to ten thousand different things, you
> know, art museums, talk about nuclear power, explain the
> eclipse.

## SKILL DEVELOPMENT

Not all employers opt for low-wage workers. Some look for caregivers who can assume highly responsible positions in their households; rather than accepting turnover, they try to structure jobs so as to minimize it. They create responsible positions of authority. These positions may go to class peers, women who are culturally similar to the parents. This arrangement does not appeal to all employers, though, partly because many class peers refuse to do all the desired tasks. Some employers who want full housework done as well as child care, and want both done by a self-starting woman, create jobs that they fill with acculturated immigrant women. With time, skill development, and English proficiency, immigrant women from Central America or the Caribbean can escape from the low-wage ghetto into these better "housekeeper" jobs.

Immigrants without legal working papers, and with little formal schooling, find many occupations are closed to them. These immigrants have better prospects for moving up in the hierarchy of domestic work, however limited that occupation might be, than of switching occupations entirely.[14] Domestic work does offer some limited upward mobility, with some workers able to secure increasingly responsible and better-rewarded jobs over time. They cannot easily upgrade their general level of education, but they can try to acquire those specific skills that win them higher wages or better working conditions in the caregiving market.

In part, achieving a housekeeper-type position depends on workers' skills. In Los Angeles and in suburban areas, caregivers move up several notches if they can drive. To caregivers, the best employers are those who allow them to develop their skills, by giving them time in the evenings to take English classes or by helping them get a driver's license and letting them use their cars. Some employers tie pay raises to skill acquisition.

Not all employers, though, want to help their employees gain skills. They may have created such routinized jobs that they prefer to stick with low-skill workers. Others might ideally prefer an English-speaking worker but might not want to give an employee regular time off to attend classes. Ironically, caregivers can be particularly unlucky if their employers speak even a fractured version of Spanish. This can make it harder for live-in workers to learn English and can reduce their employers' incentive to help them do so.

Some caregivers are bitter when long-term employers do not help them develop the skills that the employers demand. Melba, a thirty-six-year-old Salvadoran, has worked for her present employer for six years, but the employer has told Melba that she is thinking of replacing her. In an interview, the mother said she found it tiring getting her children to their activities. "You need to take them to art classes, soccer classes, piano classes, this, that, and the other thing. They require a chauffeur, so it's very hard." Melba was dismayed by the mother's plans:

> She told me that she would hire someone who spoke English and had a car. So I told her that if I didn't know how to speak English, it was because she had not given me the opportunity to learn it. If I don't have a car, it's because I can't afford it. "So what are you complaining about? If I don't know English, it's because of you," I told her.

While it is possible this is what Melba *wanted* to tell her employer rather than what she *did* tell her, the sentiment is the same in either case.

In general, Caribbean women seem to have an easier time rising to high-level housekeeping jobs than do Latina women. They have some advantages. Most come from English-speaking countries, so language is not an issue; in northeastern cities, where they are concentrated, driving is less important than in southwestern cities, such as Los Angeles, where Latina workers predominate. Usually older than Latina women when they come to the United States, they tend to be more established and confident. They are somewhat better educated (an average of eight years of schooling compared to six). And finally, as their children are usually older than the Latina workers' children, they have fewer outside demands on them as they build their careers.[15] A Jamaican woman who started at a demanding job, and then switched to one where she successfully limited her duties to child care, reports that she discusses potential concerns with her employers as issues arise. Married to an American citizen, and with her own children now grown, she recognizes that she is in a better position to stand up for herself than are many other caregivers:

> A lot of people who do child care work are single. They have to pay rent, they have kids that they need to take care of, they cannot jeopardize their job. The little they work for, they cannot make a big savings from it. They say, "I cannot leave this job, because I have my rent to pay, I have my bills to pay, and I have my kids to take care of. What if I leave and I go out there and I don't have enough reserve that I can back myself up for two or three months before I pick up a job?"

Housekeepers appreciate freedoms workers in other occupations take for granted. A caregiver from Trinidad, who has been with her Manhattan employers for five years, says the mother is not a slavemaster over her: "I'm not restricted of looking at TV, I'm not restricted of answering the phone, or making a phone call, I'm not restricted of going to the fridge, I'm not restricted of eating what I want." She invests herself in the two boys in her care, saying that for her it is deeply satisfying to "watch them grow and training them, so when they grow up, they could say, 'Well, I had a babysitter that showed me the right way, and didn't show me the wrong way.'"

Whereas many employers of low-wage immigrant workers

describe them in semi-derogatory terms,[16] expressing worry that they will steal, and sometimes seeing their abrupt departures as evidence of moral weakness, employers of workers defined as housekeepers, in contrast, are inclined to see these women as talented people who have been hindered by their circumstances. But even immigrant women who have taken on much responsibility cannot reliably count on good jobs; as members of a devalued group of workers, their status is always precarious.

## CONCLUSIONS

Employers can see advantages in hiring workers very different from themselves. They minimize their costs, and they can assign these workers almost any housecleaning or child-rearing task. Except for those with high-level housekeepers, seldom do they see their caregivers as superior workers, but they do see them as meeting their needs. The employers do not expect the caregivers to read to their children or to help develop their language skills. They foster the middle-class acculturation of their children through other means, including their own involvement and their children's attendance at preschools.

Immigrant caregivers work in the home, but do not take on parents' roles. They also, however, differ from trained caregivers who adopt what could be called a "nursery school style" of interaction with children. Researchers who study child care have concluded that "children are more likely to learn social and intellectual skills when caregivers are stimulating and educational, responsive and respectful, moderately affectionate and appropriately demanding."[17] The most socially subordinate caregivers have little capacity to be "appropriately demanding," given that they themselves are not in a position to make many demands. They also cannot necessarily be "stimulating and educational," as many of them do not speak the children's language and many are distracted by heavy housework duties.

They are always vulnerable to parents' sudden critiques on these matters, yet the parents themselves create the job structure that prevents caregivers from enhancing their own skills or, indirectly, those of the children in their charge.

For the workers themselves, low-skill child-rearing jobs can be alienating and dreary. The most dissatisfied caregivers can be young immigrant women who see themselves as being "locked up" in their employers' houses. More grim and resigned are the older immigrant women stuck in the low-wage ghetto, who have worked all their adult lives as deeply subordinate employees in other people's homes. Immigrant caregivers fare best when employers decide they do value skills and that the women they hire have more than a custodial role to play. This can require actively helping workers to develop skills, but not all employers make this commitment.

In tipping toward the "subordinate" side of the balance, and away from the "parent" side, parents reduce caregivers' investment in their children, a tradeoff many are willing to make. Other parents opt for workers more like themselves, whether European au pairs, young women from the Midwest, or Irish or British nannies. The next chapter considers the compromises and adjustments they make in hiring these workers.

# CHAPTER 3

# Choosing Similarity

Parents uncomfortable with the idea of having someone from a background radically different from theirs helping to raise their children and sharing their house will seek out caregivers who are culturally similar to them. These parents look for women who may not be subordinate, but who resemble mothers. One Los Angeles mother who hired a Swedish au pair said the young woman did everything in her absence just the way she would have done it. "You could go out of town and you knew that your child was absolutely going to have a mother substitute. She had total responsibility. I completely trusted her." The au pair could function well because "she was bright, and she knew the ways of the American culture really well."

Educated, culturally similar caregivers are available, although they make up a much smaller part of the employee pool than immigrant women from developing countries. Parents who hire class peers minimize cultural conflicts over child rearing. They also avoid creating extremes of hierarchy within their own households. To some parents, this is crucial. A New Jersey couple said they saw many Caribbean housekeepers in their neighborhood who were treated as servants. The mother said, "I just didn't feel comfortable with that at all. I didn't want to raise my child to think that there was someone that she could talk down to. It really upset me very much." These parents hired a succession of eight au pairs.

Yet parents who hire class peers also inevitably create a dilemma for themselves. Even when the employee is educated and acculturated, the caregiving job involves the personal subordination of employee to employer. When parents hire a class peer, they have to soften the master–servant nature of the relationship to make it acceptable to someone who has other options. In making the relationship more palatable, though, the parents sacrifice some of their power. They cannot assign housework freely and they cannot expect the caregiver to give their needs priority.

There are two main ways parents transform the caregiving relationship to remove some of the taint of personal subordination. With young women (and men) who are either college students or future college-students most couples practice a family-incorporation strategy. The caregiver attains some of the standing and rights of family members. The mother with the Swedish au pair said, "She was literally part of the family. And she knew everything that was going on. If someone in the family was in the hospital, she would go and visit them *for* me." These workers do not eat by themselves or just with the children. They do not spend most evenings alone in their rooms. They do not automatically abandon their social plans if their employers suddenly decide to go out.

Not all parents want to gain another quasi-family member, particularly one they may not meet prior to his or her arrival. For the nuclear family to relax its normally rigid boundaries in this way runs counter to the long-standing trend toward a narrowing of family focus.[1] Incorporating a stranger into the household takes time and emotional effort that some parents simply do not want to expend. One Los Angeles mother said of au pairs, "From what I know about them, they want a vehicle, and they want a life, and to me that was an extra responsibility, like being [their] mother." Furthermore, as semi-family members, caregivers cannot be assigned any type of work the parents do not share themselves. Work reserved only for the caregiver acquires a stigma that can make her resistant to doing it.

Parents can also help equalize relationships with class peers by founding them on a professional footing. Among British nannies, for example, some have taken special training courses for nannies, some have worked under experienced nannies in large, formally organized households, and some have participated in college or polytechnic programs in child care or child development. Professional nannies only do work directly related to children's care: They will do children's laundry, but not adult laundry; they will organize children's rooms, but not do general housekeeping. They expect to operate with considerable autonomy, to have decent accommodations, to be paid a competitive salary, and to be treated with respect. Only wealthy families can consider hiring them.

By hiring class peers, parents are minimizing distinctions between child care as they do it and as their employees do it. These caregivers operate with some authority, preparing children for a cultural world they themselves know and understand. Many of the parents who hire them see child-rearing attitudes as deeply rooted, formed by people's own experiences growing up and by their exposure to education. Believing they cannot readily change the child-rearing style of the people they hire, they seek a caregiver who naturally has ideas similar to their own. Many such parents believe that educated caregivers will actively engage their children in ways that less-educated caregivers will not. These parents see child care not as routinized drudgery, but as a high-level assignment requiring subtle skills that are part and parcel of a caregiver's entire being.

When parents have conflicts with a class peer, they are less often about child care than about other aspects of the job or the caregiver's relationship with the parents. Because class peers have greater freedom to express themselves than class subordinates do, personality conflicts can emerge strongly. More fundamentally, some parents do not follow strategies that could reduce class peers' resistance to domestic work; these parents can quickly alienate their caregivers. They create contradictory relationships, in which they expect culturally sensitive performance from class peers, but treat them as they would class subordinates.

## THE SUPPLY OF CLASS PEERS

The main types of class peers available for caregiving work are American college students, European au pairs, young women from the American Midwest, and Irish and British nannies. American college students and au pairs are essentially similar in social origin and are hired by the same types of families. Parents may hire American college students rather than au pairs because they want only native English speakers, they live near a college, or they want to avoid paying the agency fees that are required if au pairs are hired legally.

Due to immigration rules, the au pair pool is more organized than that for most other caregivers. Eight agencies have been authorized to import a specific number of au pairs each year (less than 10,000 among all the agencies). By the conditions of their visas, au pairs are not allowed to work more than forty-five hours a week. They come to the United States for cultural experience or adventure, and agencies require parents to set aside time for au pairs to attend classes. Agencies inspect accommodations offered by parents and reject employers who do not have a separate room (with a door) for the au pair. Parents pay au pairs wages that are specified by the agencies (generally $100 a week) and they also pay the agencies substantial fees, which cover administrative costs, medical insurance, and airfare. Au pairs can count on agencies for some level of protection; if they have disputes with their employers, community counselors mediate. When differences prove to be irreconcilable, au pairs can enter "rematch" programs and be sent to new employers.

Many au pairs also come to the United States illegally, entering as tourists and overstaying their visas. In some parts of northern Europe, there are extensive informal recruiting networks, with au pairs already in the United States writing friends or family members about employment opportunities. These au pairs avoid agencies for a number of reasons: They may be too young to enroll in agency programs, they may not have a driver's license (required by many agencies), or they may not be able to muster the $500 good-faith deposit required by agencies. For their part, parents have obvious financial incentives to avoid agencies. Some parents always hire illegal au pairs; some begin by working through agencies but then, as they become experienced, switch to informal recruiting; and some employers, more cautious or rule-abiding than others, always hire through agencies.

Au pairs come mainly from northern Europe (Britain, Germany, Scandinavia, and the Benelux countries). The class structure of the southern European countries yields fewer young women (and men) who are willing to exchange a year's domestic work for cultural experience. In these countries, middle- and upper-middle-class youths are likely to have been raised by servants and to be unenthusiastic about joining their ranks, even briefly. Parents in these countries may also want to keep their daughters close to home and may be unwilling to send them to completely unknown households for a year. Agencies report that English au pairs are often of a lower-social class background than are au pairs from countries such as Germany; au pairs are required to speak English reasonably well, which can serve as a kind of class litmus test for au pairs from non-English-speaking countries but obviously does not for those from Britain. Because of their higher social class, agency representatives say, German au pairs are more likely than English au pairs to explicitly discuss child-rearing issues with parents. They are more likely to have developed philosophies of their own and to be willing to articulate them.

The market for college students is completely unorganized.

No statistics exist to show the number of college students doing caregiving work. Domestic employment agencies handle students who are stepping out of school for a period and are interested in full-time work, but they do not handle students doing part-time work in exchange for room and board.

Young women from the American Midwest also form part of the caregiving market. These women, often from rural areas or small towns in states such as Iowa, Oklahoma, or Utah, work as live-in nannies. They find jobs by answering newspaper ads placed in their local papers by prospective employers or by nanny agencies. Mormon nannies are particularly popular, as parents like their wholesome reputation.[2] Midwestern women offer employers several advantages: They know how to drive; they speak English; they can, if necessary, talk with children's teachers, do the grocery shopping, or take on other aspects of care that require familiarity with American lifestyles; and they are, of course, American citizens, so no issues of legality arise. The agencies that recruit and place these women emphasize their homegrown quality, with names such as Apple Pie Agency or the All-American Child Care Agency.

The women do the work because they want to leave their home towns, but do not have the educational or economic resources to move to large cities on their own. By living in, they, like newly arrived immigrant women, avoid the need to pay rent or utilities. They can move across the country with almost no financial reserves. However, their circumstances are otherwise quite different from those of immigrant women; as a rule, they only take jobs that offer them such privileges as access to a car, freedom to pursue their social lives in the evenings, and their own rooms. They reject the most onerous forms of housework. In a sense, they are class peers by courtesy; most are not middle-class, but they gain from their ambiguous status as Americans from the heartland. They are often hired by suburban employers.

Irish nannies are the European equivalent of Midwestern nannies. They, too, tend to be from working-class or lower-middle-class backgrounds. Not able to boast specific child care training, they do domestic jobs as a way to escape from dead-end situations. They seldom drive, and most prefer city jobs. Like their Midwestern counterparts, they benefit in the market from speaking English and, agency heads report, from being white.

English nannies generally find their jobs through agencies. Despite their high status, many also enter the United States illegally. They earn vastly higher wages in the United States than they can in Britain, due both to Britain's depressed economy and to the special cachet, valuable only in America, of an English accent. Most come from upper-working-class or lower-middle-class backgrounds.

## THE PURSUIT OF "QUALITY" CARE

Parents who conclude that quality child care can best be offered by class peers equate educated caregivers with engaged caregivers. In their eyes, caregivers should act as much like parents as possible. They want caregivers who operate with confidence and authority and who turn daily activities into opportunities for learning. To them, children's socialization is not low-skill work, but demanding work that calls forth a caregiver's creativity. Many such parents comment negatively on unengaged caregivers they see around them and express relief that they have followed a different path. These parents want to transfer high-level child care duties to their caregivers. Sometimes this means the parents (particularly the mother) will perform routine tasks themselves, while the caregiver does higher-level work. These parents do not believe that servants can provide good child care; they sacrifice the benefits of having a servant in order to secure child care that meets their class-specific standard.

The goals of such parents can be seen in the experience of

a New Jersey couple, the Breslows, both doctors, who have hired a succession of college-educated American caregivers to look after their two boys, seven and ten, and a girl of four. Initially the parents hired a Jamaican immigrant, but as the children got older, the mother approached an agency with a request for a different type of caregiver: "I specified that I wanted a college-educated nanny, because at that point my kids were bigger and I thought that talking to them, homework, intellectual companionship was important." She also wanted to hire a native English speaker because her middle child has a speech delay.

Unlike employers hiring class subordinates for routinized tasks, who often see the labor pool as inexhaustible, Sandy Breslow felt she had to compete for a qualified worker. For a live-in nanny, the Breslows paid nearly $400 a week, provided a private suite on the third floor of their spacious house, supplied a car, and paid Social Security. To make sure the candidates were as good as they sounded, the Breslows, who were using an agency that placed caregivers from around the country, flew out the most promising ones and had them stay for a weekend while they watched them with the children. The hiring process was expensive and time-consuming, but worth it, Sandy felt, because it helped her avoid the situation of a friend who ran through a string of nannies, each staying only briefly. The friend's six-year-old daughter once asked, "What was the name of that nanny we rented a few weeks ago?"

Once hired, the nanny was told to organize her days around the children. She could do errands, but only if she gave them educational content. Sandy explained:

> The nanny knows that I feel the day has to be child centered. That I don't approve of taking the kids to the mall or taking the kids on errands that she's doing for herself. Anything she does, she should involve the kids, so that if they go grocery shopping, you name the fruit, you add, you subtract, you deal with not fighting in the aisles.

Sandy granted her caregivers considerable autonomy. She relied on them to be resourceful. She told them they were taking her place and she wanted the day to go the way it would have if she were home.

When asked whether the nannies did cleaning, Sandy replied, "Oh, heavens no." Sandy sometimes wonders about the tradeoff she has made. "Occasionally they'll all be outside playing baseball and I'll be cleaning the playroom and I'll say to myself, What is wrong with this picture? They're having a great time and I'm in here putting away the Legos, but it's worth it because my kids have been very happy." Annoyed when the caregiver left pots in the sink, Sandy nevertheless did them herself. "I wasn't happy about it, but I didn't want to annoy her. I didn't want to get into any power struggles, because the tradeoff was that she was exactly on my wavelength about how to handle the kids."

The Breslows' succession of caregivers did much more than routine child care. Each, for example, talked with the middle boy's speech therapist and followed the weekly program she recommended. They became so involved that each caregiver flirted with the idea of becoming a speech therapist herself.

Sandy has tried to hire independent women who have not wanted her to mother them. She does, however, try to incorporate them into the family, inviting them on outings, such as trips to museums. Sandy and her husband have enjoyed socializing with some of the caregivers, including one male English au pair. "David and I both wanted to marry him. Oh my God. He would play with the kids. He taught my older one to swim. Then he would come home and read *Barron's* [financial weekly] and discuss it." Sometimes the Breslows stayed home just so they could talk to this au pair, and they later visited him in England. In their worldview, the ideal nanny would be as interesting to them as to the children.

Despite the Breslows' success with high-level caregivers, they are now reconsidering their needs. Their children are all in school, so the Breslows are not sure they should invest in a college-educated nanny. When the children spent ten hours a day with the caregiver, Sandy and her husband thought it was worth it. Now their socialization strategy focuses on helping the children do well at school, and their money also flows in that direction: they pay three private-school tuitions.

The Breslows have high standards for the care they want their children to receive, both that offered by them, as parents, and by those they hire. They make little distinction between these two types of care, unlike parents who see their own labor as high-quality and that of paid caregivers as routine. They accept the costs of their socialization strategy. Sandy dispenses with personal leisure. She does not go out on weekday evenings, because she does not want to be away from her children and she thinks the caregiver deserves a break. She also takes on (if reluctantly) the household tasks the caregivers leave undone. She and her husband have the substantial resources required to attract the kind of caregivers they want: They pay a high salary for a live-in worker.

Only high-income parents can look to the Breslows' child care solution as a model. Parents with the same goals, but less money, can sometimes follow a basically similar strategy if they require only part-time work from a caregiver, even a live-in one. For such parents, college students become caregivers of choice, as many students desire part-time work and they have the cultural credentials the parents want.

One Los Angeles couple, with two boys, ages five and three, hired a succession of college students, offering them no wage but room and board. The mother, Stephanie Schreiber, initially did not work, then began a part-time job. The father works in the film industry. Stephanie wants caregivers who enrich the children's lives and socialize them in what she considers a culturally acceptable manner. She considers only caregivers who speak English well, as she wants them to read to the children and teach them to speak correctly. Although the Schreibers live near a community college, Stephanie hires from UCLA, because she thinks students there are more intelligent.

Several of the Schreibers' caregivers have majored in child development or related fields.

Stephanie requires her sons to spend half an hour a day reading, and the caregiver is responsible for enforcing this rule. Stephanie likes her caregivers' active engagement with her sons; she believes her employees are head and shoulders above the immigrant caregivers she sees in the park. The current caregiver, Paul, "has a personality" and her sons can connect with him because of that. Immigrant women, she says, often do not talk to the children in their charge. "I'd rather not have anybody than have this kind of a robot person just doing it because they need the money."

The Schreibers pay a price for having a caregiver with "a personality." Paul does not hesitate to express his opinions. He offers Stephanie unsolicited advice on child rearing. "I constantly give her hints like what she should or shouldn't do. Sometimes she takes it to heart, sometimes she doesn't." He tells her, for example, that the kids watch too much TV while with her. Paul believes he sets a higher standard of child care than the parents do. He views the boys as "totally out of control and obnoxious," but is proud that he has developed a good relationship with them. Whereas immigrant caregivers are often afraid to discipline the children in their charge, even if they consider them rude or disagreeable, Stephanie's most successful caregivers were actually stricter than she was, which pleased her. They had the authority to make and enforce rules in her household.

Paul offers criticism more readily than he accepts it. Stephanie once accused Paul of negligence because he had been in the next room when the younger boy fell and hit his head. This situation is the worst nightmare of Latina caregivers, but Paul dismissed the boy's injury as trivial. When the conflict escalated and Stephanie told him he had skimped on some activities with the kids, Paul retorted that she had not lived up to her end of their bargain, as she had been coming home late.

Open arguments between parents and class subordinates often presage the end of relationships, but Stephanie and Paul resolved their dispute.

The Schreibers' caregivers take up psychic space in the household, and they also take up physical space. Unlike class subordinates, who learn to fade away, the Schreibers' caregivers see common space as their own. A former student caregiver often invited his girlfriend to cook with him; the two prepared multi-course meals for themselves even while Stephanie and her husband tried to eat their own dinner in the kitchen. "She'd be making cookies for later and he'd be making spaghetti sauce and she'd be making garlic bread and at the same time we would be trying to eat dinner. It was awkward." As class peers, the Schreibers' caregivers feel entitled to maintain active social schedules despite the constraints of living in someone else's home. The Schreibers expect this and accommodate themselves to it. They allow the caregivers to have their girlfriends stay overnight, almost unheard of for employers of class subordinates.

Because the caregivers are hired to provide quality child care, Stephanie demands only minimal cleaning from them. Paul explained, though, that he does some housework to please Stephanie, because it "keeps their relationship on an equal level." Paul translates housework into a favor, of the type he might do for a friend whose house he shared. In fact, he and Stephanie have a friendly and communicative relationship; sometimes, he says, Stephanie tells him more than he wants to hear about her life and marriage. As someone on her social and educational level, he becomes privy to her emotions. He "has a personality" and she does too, and they share them with each other, not always smoothly or easily, but with some sense of mutual interest and companionship.

Like the Breslows, Stephanie is now reconsidering her socialization strategy, or at least one element of it. Her caregivers, male college students, have been spared the burden of housework not only by their class, but by their sex. Stephanie is reconsidering hiring men. She has increased her work hours, and would like to have a caregiver do more housework. "The last two guys that were here, I just didn't feel comfortable asking them to clean up as much as I would if a female was living here. I think girls will just do things without being asked. Men, you know. . . . " She explained that she ended up doing Paul's laundry; she didn't actually resent it, but did think it should have been the other way around.

Like the Breslows, who said they always had the best nanny in the neighborhood, Stephanie said she has better-quality child care than anyone she knows, even those who pay $500 a week. And, like Sandy Breslow, Stephanie gets the quality of care she wants by investing much of her own time in the children's care and housework. Stephanie gives up the advantage of class power over a caregiver for the advantage of cultural similarity; she cannot ask her caregivers to get lost, she can't make them withhold their opinions, and she can't make them suppress their social lives. She accepts these costs more readily than her husband, but he has gone along with her hiring strategy.

Particularly in Los Angeles, where a vast and ever-replenished pool of workers from Mexico and Central America makes it easy to hire immigrants at low wages, parents who hire class peers are doing the unusual. In the pull between the parents' immediate interests (reduced housework) and long-term goals (child rearing in their own image), they opt for the latter.

## RACIAL PREJUDICE

The Screibers and Breslows have made the education levels of their caregivers a hiring criterion. For some parents, another element enters into their hiring choices, a distaste not only for uneducated caregivers but also for those of other races and ethnicities. They want their children socialized by those who are like themselves in terms of ethnicity as well as class. This automatically removes the bulk of caregivers from consideration. Black and Latina workers exist for these parents mainly as members of devalued groups and cultures.

The history of domestic workers shows that dominant groups consider members of economically and socially subordinate groups to be suitable to do their menial labor.[3] Some employers, though, take their negative attitudes toward subordinates so far that they do not even want them to do menial work. In the American Southwest, for example, Mexican-American women long supplied domestic workers for Anglo employers, but some employers refused to hire them.[4] There is a complex issue here: While some white employers who are racially prejudiced may prefer black or Latina workers, as they believe their own racial identity is thereby affirmed, others may want to be surrounded only by workers of their own race. Judith Rollins points out that "the issue of ethnic and racial preference is not a simple one in domestic service. There are strong indications that many employers prefer whites for childcare, in particular."[5]

Some employers begin with prejudiced ideas but then change their minds. This was true of a Santa Monica employer, who hired her first caregiver when she had to return to work two days after her daughter's birth. She hired an older white woman who lived in a rich neighborhood of Santa Monica. The caregiver explained that she was looking for extra income because her children had started college. The mother said candidly she hired this woman for racial reasons. "I was a lot younger and dumber and inexperienced then, but basically, and I am ashamed to say this, it was racial bias." Having grown up in a Midwestern city where she attended all-white schools, she had no experience with minorities. She said she was afraid to hire a black person or a Hispanic person to take care of her baby. These racial attitudes coalesced with class ones. Impressed by "this nice lady with an English accent" who lived in an affluent suburb, the mother said, "I just thought, Oh perfect, high class, high tone."

The mother was quickly disillusioned. The caregiver refused

to pick the baby up when she was crying, saying that she did not intend to respond to the baby's every demand. She also smoked in the baby's presence. The father still refers to her as the witch. The parents replaced her with their Salvadoran housecleaner, who stayed with them for seven years.

Other employers have more firmly rooted racial prejudices. They do not see minority caregivers as suitable companions for their children or for themselves. When her son was very young, Ellen Merton thought Latina caregivers were adequate: "I had non-English-speaking Hispanic help, and that was okay as long as Josh couldn't talk, but as soon as he started to talk I just could not handle having someone who couldn't speak English." Ellen disliked having caregivers she considered unskilled and uneducated. "I had a couple of these really kind of seriously illiterate [caregivers]. They couldn't drive, couldn't do any-thing." She decided to hire class peers instead: "I had Swedish girls for about six years, and these Swedish girls are wonderful, middle-class, European kids. They speak English, they're well educated, they're bright, they're well mannered. I have just been so happy with that system of child care."

When Ellen first switched to hiring class peers, she had retained a Mexican weekly cleaning woman. But, having rid herself of class subordinates as child care workers, Ellen next decided to go a step further and get rid of them as cleaners. "But then I got so sick of these cleaning ladies. I really don't like the non-English-speaking, Hispanic, surly mentality, I don't like it at all." She wanted class peers across the entire house-hold front. She didn't want Latina cleaners because, she said, they were a "foreign presence, and I don't like it." Clearly the issue was not foreign or nonforeign in terms of nationality, as the au pairs were also from other countries, but foreign in terms of class and ethnicity. Sonia, their current caregiver, a Hungar-ian, commented that the husband had not liked having Latina women handle his things.

When Josh started school, his parents sent him to the local

public school. This school is unusual in that it enrolls many high-income children, as well as having a significant population of low-income minority students, who are bused in. The parents decided not to send Josh to the public middle school. There was a limit to how much minority exposure Ellen wanted him to have. The junior high

> has gangs and stuff. It's icky. I don't want him to go there. The busing situation is one thing when the kids are five, six, and seven, and they're little and they're cute and they're innocent, but when they hit puberty and they start becoming gang members and stuff . . . I only have one kid, I'm just not going to do it.

## THE AU PAIR'S PERSPECTIVE

We also interviewed the caregiver in this family, who provided her own perspective. Sonia, a twenty-four-year-old Hungarian with two years of college, thinks she has "the best job around." The daughter of a doctor, Sonia hated her first caregiving job in the United States, where the employers "did not have any idea who I was" and treated her like a servant. The Mertons, however, understand her background: "They see who I am and appreciate that." Sonia likes Ellen and says they get along well. "She's a very interesting person. I'm my own person and she's her own person."

Although Sonia likes her job, she is amazed at the level of service the family demands, particularly the father and son. The father, she said, was particularly helpless. "This is scary. It's like he really couldn't find a knife or a fork himself at home. You go into the kitchen in the morning, I mean, they can't put their coffee cup into the dishwasher, which is a real simple procedure." Most class subordinates accept the idea that people wealthier than they are want personal service. But Sonia rejects this notion. She would never invite an employee to live in her home. "To be dependent on some other person in your own family life, that's weird, really weird."

To Sonia, the parents' strategy of hiring caregivers to focus on Josh is fundamentally faulty, because it has led Josh, age ten, to become dependent and aggressive. He looks to others to entertain and energize him. "I wasn't bored when *I* was a child! But he has more toys than our kindergarten probably had and he's constantly bored!" He can be explosively bad-tempered. At summer camp he kicked someone so badly he caused internal bleeding. When Sonia first arrived, he kicked her. "But, you know, I don't take that! *No* ten-year-old is going to kick me." The most socially subordinate caregivers have a hard time controlling aggressive children of Josh's age. Too self-confident to be cowed, Sonia laughed at the idea that a child his age would try to control her. She worries that Josh lacks "patience and tolerance" and does not think he has been helped by his ever-changing succession of nannies.

Ellen describes her son as very bright. She interprets his frequent boredom as a sign of his intelligence. At camp, she said, he hated the "stupid" games they were forced to play. Sonia sees the matter quite differently. Beyond protecting herself, though, she does not attempt to intervene, believing that it would be impossible for her to resocialize Josh without active support from the parents. She has struggled to get him to help out around the house, but finds it an uphill battle. "I can go only so far, I can't go further. You can't do it without the parents."

Sonia never finds the job tedious, because it has taught her about "relationships and sacrifice." She hopes to study psychology at UCLA and realizes her work gives her much opportunity to observe family dynamics. Sonia also considers the job manageable because even though she is a live-in employee, she can limit her hours. The parents separated while Sonia was there, and when the father arrived late for his weekend visits with his son, Sonia told him his tardiness was unacceptable. "I've confronted him. I've told him that I'm ready to help if I can, but if I make plans, then I expect that I can fulfill my plans."

Sonia also made her own decision about cleaning the house. When the family fired the Mexican cleaning woman, Sonia took on the housework in exchange for getting half her tuition paid at the local community college.

Sonia is bolstered by a strong sense that she is not truly a domestic employee. She sees the job as strictly temporary, emphasizing that she doesn't hang around with other nannies and has not joined a "nanny club." Her family in Hungary marvels that she has entered domestic work: "My family still doesn't believe that I do it. My mother said, 'You'll be fired the next day, I mean, you can't clean or cook.'" While Sonia may not have been raised with domestic skills, she has translated her general cultural capital into a relatively privileged form of domestic employment.

In hiring Sonia, Ellen obtained an independent, educated woman with a strong sense of herself. Unintimidated even by an aggressive, willful child with a long history of having nannies to do things for him, she does not allow the parents' or the child's demands to demoralize her. She does not view Josh's aggression as her problem, but as his. Similarly, secure in her identity as a member of the upper middle class herself, she does not feel stigmatized by the parents' demands for personal service, but sees it as the parents' failure to be independent. For her, it "is sad, totally sad," but no reflection on her.

Ellen has created a racially and socially homogeneous environment for Josh at home and she wants the same for him at school. Ellen associates minorities with menace and surliness. Accepting, and reinforcing, inequalities along lines of race and gender, the mother thinks Josh has adapted well to having young women hired "for him," not sharing Sonia's sense that the family is reproducing a pattern of learned helplessness and expectation of privilege.

## FAMILY-INCORPORATION STRATEGIES

Most parents who hire class peers try to mobilize their employees' emotional commitment, by providing a familylike setting for them. They do this both by extending themselves personally to the au pairs and by assigning them work that does not differ in kind from that taken on by the parents.

The parents for whom family-incorporation strategies are easiest tend to be open, flexible, and informal. They strive to create not a hierarchy but an egalitarian and friendly relationship. Within such a framework, they can delegate significant amounts of work to the caregiver. Class peers can feel they are doing the work semi-voluntarily, as contributing members of a family system.

Au pairs comment favorably about alternating tasks with parents. Karoline, a German au pair, values her close relationship with the mother who employs her. "It is kind of best friends and mother and daughter, it's both. I don't feel like a stranger or like a worker." She and the mother have similar tastes in food and clothing. She thinks the parents have a good relationship with each other and with their six-year-old son. "They're happy, they're laughing, they're singing, they're listening to music, they're sitting in front of the TV together. That's what I really love here." Karoline said she did not even like to use the word "work" to describe what she did in the family. Most class peers in successful relationships see their work as transcending duty and being performed out of friendship and family feeling.

Child care involves a multitude of tiny tasks, each individually easy but adding up to what can be exhausting labor over the course of a day. While gross cases of neglect by caregivers are rare, neglect can also take place in small ways. Parents cannot prevent this in their absence, but hiring self-motivated workers can reduce its likelihood. Parents who foster family feeling with class peers are essentially striving to ensure conscientiousness by developing personal bonds.

In fact, few of the parents interviewed complained about how college students or au pairs treated their children (although one case of neglect was reported). Because these caregivers come from the same broadly defined cultural background as the parents, in terms of being from educated classes in industrialized nations, they seldom have fundamental value disagreements. A community representative for an au pair agency in New Jersey reported that out of the hundred or so families where she has placed au pairs, only two have had problems regarding the employees' relations with the children. Au pairs often do consider the children spoiled, and they are surprised by how dependent they are, shepherded by adults and unable to go around neighborhoods freely. Coming from less violent societies, the American emphasis on safety requires considerable adjustment for them. Some also are surprised by the occasional rudeness with which children talk to their parents; they are not surprised by the amount of conversation, but can be startled by its nature. Most au pairs adapt, aided by orientation programs operated by their agencies. Like Sonia, the Hungarian caregiver, they do not tend to take children's behavior as personally as do some class subordinates, who can become the targets of status putdowns in a way that middle-class caregivers cannot.

Conflicts more often arise between the au pairs and the parents. Families attract class peers by suggesting they offer more than a job, they offer a slice of middle-class American life, a prospect that is particularly appealing for European au pairs. The quid pro quo involves skilled labor in exchange for a cultural experience in an emotionally sheltered environment. Parents cannot or do not always deliver on this promise. Some are too preoccupied with pursuing their demanding careers; some families have negative internal relationships and cannot easily incorporate anyone.

Some parents hire au pairs, but do not accept the basic principle of the au pair relationship, the idea of equality between parent and caregiver. While au pair agencies tout the cultural exchange element of their programs, some parents see au pairs as cheap labor. They assign them household tasks they do not wish to do themselves. When this occurs, however, au pairs have more recourse than do immigrant caregivers. They can count on at least some help from their agencies in mediating disputes, and if problems persist, they can switch families.

Alexandra, a Norwegian au pair, works for a New Jersey family with two boys, ages ten and thirteen. She resents the housework she is assigned. She is constantly on call during the day and has to perform many personal tasks for the mother, including organizing her closets. Alexandra eats dinner with the family, but she does not find it a pleasant experience. And as soon as the meal is over, Alexandra reverts to the role of servant. She, and only she, clears the table, puts the dishes in the dishwasher, and cleans the kitchen.

A Swedish au pair, Ingrid, had a similar problem. She worked for an extremely wealthy New Jersey family with three boys, ages fourteen, thirteen, and eleven. Both parents ran their own businesses. They left home at 7 in the morning and did not return until late in the evening. Ingrid worked fourteen or fifteen hours a day, from 7 A.M. until 10 or 10:30 P.M. six days a week. Her duties included waking the boys in the morning, taking them to activities, supervising their homework, and cooking and serving their meals. In the two months she stayed with the family, she ate dinner with the parents only once. The parents hardly ever spent time with their children, who were hostile and challenging. When Ingrid told them to go to bed, the oldest boy would reply, "Fuck you, bitch."

The parents did no work of any kind around the huge house, which had eight bathrooms, a gym, and a Jacuzzi. They employed a Jamaican housekeeper as well as Ingrid, but the house was so big there was work for both women. Ingrid organized the family's possessions and ran errands, while the housekeeper did the cleaning. Ingrid and the housekeeper struck up a friendship, but the parents told Ingrid not to talk with her because she was black. The housekeeper was not allowed to interact with the children.

When Ingrid complained to the agency that had brought her to the United States, the mother became angry. She ordered Ingrid to leave the house within half an hour, which she did. No one in the family said good-bye to her. The parents went through four more au pairs before being cut off by the agency.

Ingrid thought the basic problem with the family was that the parents did not get along well with each other. To avoid each other, they avoided being home. There was no family life into which an au pair could be incorporated. The parents wanted their children socialized by educated white caregivers, but once this basic requirement was met, they withdrew from all further involvement.

Both Ingrid's and Alexandra's employers treated au pairs like servants and assigned them chores they would not do themselves. Au pair agencies try to convince employers this will not work. Other, more subtle problems can arise even when parents do actively want to mobilize their employees' emotions. The family-incorporation strategy rests on having people of the right personality and culture to be incorporated.

Parents who have employed large numbers of au pairs almost always have had at least a few whose company they did not particularly enjoy. Sometimes they actively disliked them. Highly withdrawn au pairs can be a problem, as they offer parents little visible reward for struggling to incorporate them. Outgoing au pairs or students tend to do best. The ideal personality for a class peer differs from the ideal personality for a class subordinate, as parents have different degrees of interaction with them: unobtrusiveness is valued in subordinates but not in peers.

Parents and caregivers tend to become closest when they feel they are similar in important respects. Some employers are open to close relationships, but may not like the character or tastes of their particular au pairs. While they would not expect much cultural similarity with a class subordinate, with a peer they might expect more similarity than may actually exist. One employer was disheartened when his English au pair did not want to see the sights of New York. He found her intellectually inert. A Los Angeles lawyer criticized her Scottish au pair:

> She wasn't a personality type that I would be proud of if she was my daughter. On her time off, her favorite thing to do was to walk up Rodeo Drive [in Beverly Hills]. I tried to show her that there were other things to do and she really had absolutely no interest. All she wanted to do was buy a certain number of things. She thought certain TV shows were critically important.

The employer was also startled at how badly educated the au pair was. She did not conceal her dismay or her sense that the au pair was culturally deficient.

> I remember we were cooking together, and she didn't even know fractions. It said a half a cup and we had poured in a quarter of a cup and I said pour in the rest, and she said, I don't know how much to measure out. So I said, "are you kidding me? You mean, you don't understand?" And she said, "well, my dad always did my math papers." I said, "well, it doesn't really help you now, does it?"

Au pairs' social lives can cause parents much anxiety; because the parents see these caregivers as quasi-family members, they worry about them as they would their own teenage children. Parents get disturbed when au pairs stay out until four and get drunk. Some parents try to control caregivers' schedules, on the grounds that they cannot function well with the children if they are exhausted, but most recognize they have to accept the caregivers' right to a social life, a right many class subordinates are not able to claim.

Some parents try to impose restrictions on au pairs during the workday, which can lead to their angry departures. One Swedish au pair, from a more working-class background than most, had worked for a New Jersey couple with a new baby for five months, during which time the parents had not once allowed her to take the baby out, even to a playground or the corner store. The parents said they did not want the baby to mingle with other children until she was two years old. The au pair arrived at the apartment at 7 in the morning and stayed until 5 or 6 at night. The parents did not ask her to do housework, so she had nothing to occupy her besides baby care. The TV and phone were the au pair's lifelines. She felt imprisoned in the apartment, almost insanely bored. She hadn't gone through an agency, so she had no support. She had, however, developed a plan. She said that "I can take a lot until it's getting enough, and then I'm getting revenge." The au pair planned to leave a message on the parents' answering machine saying (falsely) that she had gone back to Sweden.

Another Swedish au pair worked for a dual-career Manhattan couple who objected to her taking their baby out for hours every day. The au pair replied that she got depressed if she spent all day indoors. The agency representative tried to negotiate a compromise, where the au pair could go out for a certain period each day. The parents rejected the compromise. The mother said, "I don't care about her well-being. Her job is taking care of my kid." They fired the au pair and hired a Jamaican caregiver in her place. The mother said that after their experience with the au pair, they asked the Jamaican woman if she had strong ideas about how she wanted to do things. "And she said that she had ideas but she was pretty flexible and thought the parents knew best how to take care of their kid." Reassured, they are pleased to have switched from a class peer to a class subordinate.

## THE PROFESSIONAL MODEL

The family-incorporation strategy does not work for parents who are not willing to share their lives with semi-strangers or who do not want to share workloads. Some of these parents, though, do want to hire class peers. They can do so if they hire educated workers who see themselves as professionals, such as British nannies. This option is available only to the wealthy. English nannies can earn $600 or $700 a week. Some receive extensive perks, including full job benefits, much travel, and even their own apartments.

Having secured the most elite form of child care for their offspring, some employers of British nannies spend very little time in the home. Sharon, an English nanny, worked for a Manhattan couple who both held jobs in the finance industry. She looked after their two children, a two-year-old and a baby; the baby slept in Sharon's room. The mother left home at 6:30 every morning and returned at 7 at night. The father was gone from 8 A.M. to 8 P.M. each day. Sharon had complete responsibility for the children's care. She liked having this high level of autonomy. "It actually felt like I was the mum, that I was in total control of everything." During the summers, Sharon and the two children spent close to two months in Nantucket. The parents joined them on weekends.

When parents hire a credentialed professional, their flexibility in asking the caregiver to take on additional tasks can be reduced, as exemplified by a Los Angeles couple, both lawyers, whose English nanny, an older woman, brought a confident kind of order to the household. The mother, warm and deeply attached to her eighteen-month-old daughter, was conflicted about her own long work hours. She did not want to give up the position she had attained as a respected tax lawyer with interesting cases, but she resented having to leave her daughter for most of each day. She partially resolved this tension by hiring a caregiver in whom she had complete confidence.

The nanny, who had great authority within the household, instructed the mother in how to raise the child. The mother accepted this and thought hiring the nanny had been the best thing she had ever done. She was worried, though, because she was pregnant with a second child and the nanny was not sure she could shift her attention from the older child. The mother decided to hire a second nanny. The nanny then reconsidered, saying that she could deal with two children if she had extra help, perhaps a subordinate employee. The parents' high incomes made it easier for them to accept the nanny's requirements: they have a very large house (eight bedrooms), so it was possible to consider an additional live-in employee, and they hired a cleaning woman so the nanny did not have to take on household responsibilities. The mother was considering hiring yet another employee to handle grocery shopping.

The content of the professional care offered by English nannies may or may not appeal to education-conscious parents. Most English nannies stress that they can help children learn and that this is part of their jobs. Old-line professional nannies, however, can emphasize schedule and structure to the exclusion of playful involvement with children. This has less appeal to most middle-class American parents.

A Los Angeles lawyer married to a lawyer hired first a French nanny and then an English one. When the French nanny arrived, the mother told her about some of the games she liked to play with the baby. The nanny replied that she was not a mother and did not really play with a baby the way a mother would. The nanny refused to do any cleaning, and the mother found her standoffish and cold. The mother replaced her with the English nanny, who took the baby on two-hour walks in the stroller. The mother told this nanny that she thought her child needed conversation and more varied experiences. She explained that her idea of good child care involved active participation with the baby, not "strapping her into a stroller and treating her as a blob." The nanny replied that in England it was a sign of status to have a baby with color in its cheeks. The mother fired her. Few educated American parents would pay a premium for professional care so irrelevant to their main concerns. Most English nannies, though, recognize the preoccupations of American parents and stress their ability to foster children's cognitive skills.

## CONCLUSIONS

At first glance, it would seem that hiring class peers would ensure that children were more or less automatically socialized into the parents' own values and way of life. Many parents do adopt child care strategies based on this straightforward notion. The actual implementation of such strategies, though, turns out to be more complex than many parents at first envision. There is a fundamental contradiction between acquiring a self-motivated, educated employee and placing her in a subservient position. The parents must be willing to share more of their own class resources with their employee, and to cede more of their power, than they would with a class subordinate. They partially lose the advantage of their social position in gaining the advantage of the caregiver's.

Even those parents who operate successfully for years with class peers note that their employees sometimes convey their belief that they are doing the parents a favor. Sandy Breslow said that she had almost always succeeded in getting self-directed caregivers who brought insight and creativity to their jobs, but the tradeoff was that they were all at some point a little too good for the job. For class peers, domestic work involves an exchange of favors and rewards, as opposed to the more routinized forms of labor.

With subordinates, parents can decide quite freely which tasks to assign to them. They are limited not by the employee's veto power so much as by the employee's perceived incapacity to perform some culturally sensitive tasks. Class peers, in contrast, have the potential to handle almost the full range of child-rearing tasks performed by the parents, raised as they have been in worlds with some similarity to the parents' own. Yet the very upbringing that gave them the capacity to fulfill these requests also makes them unwilling to do many of the jobs their employers might wish to transfer to them.

In addition, when parents hire class peers they are hiring

people who expect to express their personalities. They are adding another human being to their household who cannot be treated as if she or he had no individuality. While class subordinates are often treated by their employers as functional, but not expressive, those caregivers who are culturally similar to the parents anticipate that their individuality will be acknowledged. They cannot be dismissed or shoved to the margins of the parents' lives in the way that class subordinates can be and often are.

The emotional and economic costs of hiring class peers vary with parents' circumstances. Overall, value similarity does not come cheaply.

# CHAPTER 4

# The Struggle for Control

Unlike workers who supply other services, a child care worker has only one employer. This means she can be uniquely sensitive to that employer's needs. It also means, though, that she can be peculiarly vulnerable and that there are no buffers between employer and employee. Professionally skilled as they may be, most parents have no experience at directing an employee in their own home. While they have advantages of money and power, they have to learn how to translate these into effective personal control of a caregiver. This can be daunting for some new employers. A Los Angeles psychologist said that when she hired her first caregiver, "I didn't have a clue. I remember when she first came, if the baby was asleep it would be like, Oh, dear, what can I have her do now?"

As with other elements of privilege, what can be seemingly automatically accomplished by a class as a whole—the domination of domestic employees by their middle-class employers—can be problematic for individuals and does not take place without effort. Getting the labor they want from the employees they want can be a fraught and difficult process.

Parents hope caregivers will come to love their children or at least become fond of them. Unlike most jobs, where performance can be evaluated according to objective criteria, caregiving involves hard-to-measure personal commitment. When parents ask caregivers to transcend specific work obligations, it opens them to caregivers' expectations that they too will transcend their roles as employers. They can find themselves embroiled in their caregivers' crises. As one mother said about her Salvadoran caregiver, "She's got a lot of problems that come into our household." With class subordinates, this can mean parents end up serving as social safety nets, and with class peers, as emotional resources.

In hiring people to ease their lives, parents can find they have also complicated them; the flip side of personal service is personal dependence, a dependence that can mean a drain on money, time, and emotions. When a woman spends ten hours a day with their children, parents may feel obligated to help her when she asks them to. They may also feel resentful.

This chapter explores the problems parents face in learning to become employers and the dilemmas and tensions that can arise for them as they seek to direct their employees. Parents try different ways of controlling their caregiver, but whatever strategy they use, parents are far better at controlling peripheral aspects of her work than at controlling its core, the relationship between the caregiver and the child. Despite employers' efforts to supervise and motivate caregivers, they cannot really know what caregivers do with their children all day, much less control it.

## HOW PARENTS LEARN TO BE EMPLOYERS

In earlier eras, members of the upper classes expected to have servants and were taught how to hire and manage them. These skills of command are not widely dispersed in the contemporary United States, even among those who grew up privileged. Most parents we interviewed said that they did not how to approach hiring their first employee and did not know what tasks to assign her. They described latching on to recommendations by friends or family members, treating them as gospel, and imagining that the woman they hired was the only good person available. It was not common for parents to conduct systematic searches or to compare competing candidates. A Los Angeles professor said she found a Guatemalan caregiver through her personal network. "We interviewed her for probably ten minutes and hired her. I didn't know what on earth I was doing."

Some parents look back ruefully on their first choices. When she decided to return to work soon after her daughter's birth, a New Jersey doctor, feeling desperate, hired a young French woman sight unseen. The woman proved to be unstable, knew no English, and had drug-using friends. The mother commented, "In retrospect, I can't believe that I left my newborn child alone with this woman. I would never do it now. I've learned through the years to be more careful."

Over time, parents learn what they want in a caregiver and hone their interviewing skills accordingly. At first, parents can be acutely uncomfortable having an employee in the house. For those with egalitarian ideologies, employing a domestic worker can be awkward or embarrassing. They feel nervously aware of the caregiver. Several mothers said that at first they were embarrassed to take naps, afraid their caregivers would think they were lazy. Hardened employers seldom worry about what their caregivers think of them. Gradually parents become more confident and assertive. A New Jersey pediatrician, the mother of three, summed up her progression: "I just became much more defined in what I expected of someone and what I wanted done and how it should be done and what the job was. And I became a lot more firm in being able to say, I'm not happy with this, I want this done, and this has to take priority over that."

Others also said they learned they had to be explicit about what they wanted. Sometimes this involves denigration of the caregiver. A mother who does freelance desktop publishing hired a Kenyan immigrant. At first the mother was disappointed in her: "I wasn't used to having somebody do all the things I do and I guess my assumption was that she would know how to do most things. Once I realized she needed instruction, then I was able to give it. I was a little premature in judging; I thought she was stupid." The mother decided the real problem was her own inexperience as an employer (although later she candidly admitted, "But I didn't pay for bright").

Parents' adjustment speeds up as they start to enjoy the advantages of having someone to do their work. As one Los Angeles mother said, "It was kind of uncomfortable to have someone living in our house. But boy, we sure got used to it quick." Although the management of domestic employees is no longer part of the cultural knowledge transmitted in the middle class, new employers become part of networks that informally discuss and advise on these matters. One Los Angeles mother planned to invite her children's caregiver to eat meals with them; her sister-in-law advised her not to, saying that she would not be able to later disinvite her. Usually the advisers recommend being tougher with employees. They counter tendencies toward doubt and guilt or any weakening of the class fiber.

## UNCERTAIN EMPLOYERS

In some situations, parents do not ever gain confidence in directing their caregivers. New mothers can defer to experienced older women who know about baby care, and then find it hard to change this initial pattern of deference. In both good and bad relationships of this type, mothers can come to feel they are the subordinate parties.

Sometimes mothers feel partially pushed aside from the beginning. This happened to a New Jersey mother whose first caregiver was a cheerful, confident nineteen-year-old Mormon from Salt Lake City who was used to looking after her younger

brothers and sisters. The new mother said that she had not fig-
ured out how to divide tasks between them. She had not left
herself enough time alone with the baby.

> She [the caregiver] was just a little too aggressive. The first
> thing she did when she came into the house was, "Oh,
> there's the baby," and she would pick him up and so I sort
> of felt like he was being taken away from me. The cost was
> an emotional one for me, just feeling that my role was being
> usurped a little bit.

Despite liking the caregiver, the mother made sure she arranged
matters differently when she hired her successor a year later.

Another New York mother, a lawyer who, along with her
printer husband, has a history of political involvement, had a
similar experience. Her cleaning woman, a Barbadian immigrant, asked whether she could look after the baby, and the
mother agreed. The cleaning woman proved to be an outstanding caregiver and a lively, pleasant companion. Although the
mother has a forceful personality, she deferred to the caregiver
because of her greater experience with babies. She also did not
want to treat her employee in the domineering way her mother
had treated a long-term black servant. When her second baby
was born, however, the mother did not want to continue defer-
ring to her employee. Despite mixed feelings, she was ultimately relieved when the caregiver decided to become a nurse's
aide. This avoided the problem she anticipated: "I knew Ellie
would take over and I knew that there would be a competition."

The mother did not find a replacement for Ellie easily,
though. She tried an older Jamaican woman with high-level
qualifications, a former trainer of child care workers. The
mother could not influence her:

> I felt like nothing I said mattered to her. Whether it was
> about housework or the kids, she was just going to do what
> she thought best anyway. I think what she wanted was that

when I walked out, I would leave all decisions to her. While I did that with Ellie, I didn't feel like I wanted to do that with her.

The mother had passed the stage where she wanted to follow the caregiver's lead. The mother and the new caregiver parted ways.

As parents become more experienced, they reject job candidates who strike them as too assertive. A Los Angeles mother who had been willing to listen to her first caregiver's advice on how to handle her baby weeded out candidates who had strong opinions when selecting a subsequent caregiver. She interviewed an older white American woman who complained about the kids still being up at 8:30 P.M. "She said, 'These kids really should go to bed.' And that was when she lost out on the job."

Sometimes a caregiver's assertiveness with a new mother can take a more negative turn. A Manhattan mother, Carol Goodman, who worked as a commercial artist, hired Bertha, a baby nurse who was a Jamaican immigrant, to help with her first baby. "I remember when we brought Benjamin home there was like an hour and a half before she showed up, and Steve and I didn't know how to diaper him, we didn't know what to do. We were so nervous," Carol recalled. "And then she showed up and it was such a relief to have her. She was so confident." Carol believed her baby would benefit from being around someone strong and loving. The baby nurse seemed to fit the bill. For their part, the Goodmans paid an above-average wage and also covered Social Security, unemployment comp, and disability.

Bertha won an early skirmish with the parents. They had stipulated she would do light housework. "But on the first day she looked so disgruntled with the idea that we dropped that," Carol said. The parents understood that as a baby nurse, and an American citizen, Bertha might feel entitled to say no to cleaning. And unlike many caregivers who are class subordinates, Bertha did not feel she had to retreat to her room in the evenings. She watched TV in the living room. "I'd be stuck in

the bedroom," Carol said. Seeking to avoid conflict, and hating
the feeling of being "a slaveowner," Carol deferred to Bertha.
"She was very intimidating. Looking back, most of the time I
bit my lip and she ruled the roost." Carol and her husband had
heard how hard it was to get household help and they did not
want to lose their experienced caregiver.

Despite the Goodmans' initial faith in Bertha, problems
surfaced. The Goodmans always kept a bottle of vodka in the
freezer. They were surprised one evening to find that it had
frozen. Carol realized Bertha must have watered the bottle.
Three times, they spoke to her about her drinking. Carol generally avoided conflict with her, though, because when angered,
Bertha would refuse to speak to her for whole days. Carol considered firing her. Her therapist, however, advised against it,
saying continuity of care was more important for her son than a
conflict-free life was for her.

Carol found dealing with Bertha traumatic. She retained
her, though, for seven years, mainly because Bertha and her son
had a loving relationship. But Carol found her own relationship
with Benjamin becoming more distant. When the boy was two
or three, he once referred to his mother as "fucking bitch
Goodman." Carol and her husband assumed he had overheard
Bertha referring to Carol this way.

In each of these cases, it was mothers who felt encroached
upon by caregivers (even when they liked the caregivers). The
fathers had less reason to feel threatened, as their roles were not
at issue. One Los Angeles mother summed up the sense that
she, as a mother, lost her role to her first caregiver. She hired a
Salvadoran woman more or less blindly, having no idea even
what questions to ask her. The woman turned out to be very
competent at dealing with the employers' children. The mother
said, "When I was home I didn't feel comfortable, because she
had the situation so well taken care of. I wasn't feeling like the
mother, I felt more like the father." Another mother, a doctor
in Los Angeles, with children ages three and two, whose husband is also a doctor, hired two caregivers with overlapping

schedules. She said that without them, she "would have zero chance for a career." But then she added, "Sometimes I feel that it's hypocritical to call myself a parent. I feel more like I'm a visiting aunt."

Caregivers can also acquire considerable power when they work in dysfunctional families. Caregivers who end up in households where one of the parents is an alcoholic, a drug addict, or is mentally ill sometimes stay much longer than they want to, out of pity for the children. Their jobs can become highly unpleasant, as disturbed people are seldom considerate employers. Authority relations become confused; caregivers shoulder the actual burdens of running the households, but can be subject to capricious orders. Even the most committed caregivers will not stay in such situations indefinitely, but those who have endured them say that they never love children as much as those they look after in these circumstances. The caregivers both feel intensely needed and have de facto authority.

## EMPLOYER–EMPLOYEE CONFLICT

Most ordinary, functional employers gain skill and confidence in dealing with their employees. They learn, in the words of one, to cut their losses. Some never doubt their right to command others and act swiftly in the face of even seemingly minor challenges. One New Jersey mother fired an au pair on the first day because she baked a cake; the mother had told her not to turn on the stove until she had explained its operation. A Los Angeles mother lost patience with her long-term Salvadoran caregiver when the woman rearranged the living room furniture. Another employer fired a German au pair when she took the dog on a walk and it got in a fight. The same employer fired another caregiver for refusing to wash the dog's blanket. Such employers have no doubts about who should be running their houses. They can wage fierce symbolic battles, like the

Los Angeles mother who took a caregiver to small claims court over a $70 phone bill.

Decisive or ruthless employers avoid the prolonged agonies that can afflict the more delicate or sensitive. Those who are averse to conflict and ideologically committed to egalitarian relationships can become tangled in painful disputes. They are not armored by the conviction that they have the right to order others about and to be unchallenged. Some see themselves as constitutionally unsuited to be employers. A Los Angeles oncologist, self-assured in her work life, has little confidence when it comes to dealing with her caregiver, a sixty-year-old African-American woman: "I don't like doing it. I'm very uncomfortable. I'm a bad manager. Sometimes I get mad at myself for what I have allowed her to pull off."

The situation is worse for parents who have entered open conflict with caregivers. A Manhattan doctor had a disagreement with her Irish caregiver which quickly turned personal. The caregiver had taken her charge out of the apartment, although the mother had expressly asked her not to do so since the boy had earlier had a fever. The mother, a soft-spoken woman, had tolerated criticism from the caregiver about the boy's delayed toilet training, but stood her ground on a medical issue. When the mother remonstrated with the caregiver, the woman replied angrily, "I'm not your slave." Their conversation degenerated and the mother fired the caregiver. She said the open conflict "was one of the most stressful things I've ever had in my life. I think about it all the time."

A Los Angeles family became embroiled in a convoluted battle between two caregivers that caused them enormous stress. The employers hired two Guatemalan women who split the week. Although related, the two feuded bitterly. The newer employee began edging out the older one, who responded with hysteria. The mother said, "It was like living in a Guatemalan soap opera." A polite and diffident Englishwoman, the mother did not know how to quell the disturbance in her household. Finally the mother fired the more agitated of the two caregivers, who then initiated a worker's compensation suit against her for mental stress. Mulling over the situation, the mother blamed herself for not taking charge.

Middle-class people customarily avoid face-to-face confrontations. They routinely refer disputes to specialists, including police, lawyers, and public officials.[1] At work, they deal with bureaucratic infighting more often than open attack. Caregivers offer a personal service, and battles can immediately become personal. No regulations deflect or channel conflict. Disputes also can acquire an extra edge from class and racial tensions operating beneath the surface.

## FATHERS' AUTHORITY

Mothers provide most of the daily supervision of caregivers, but in some households fathers are brought in as authority figures. Several mothers said they thought the caregivers were afraid of their husbands. Some Latina caregivers call mothers by their first names but refuse to do so with fathers. One Los Angeles mother relied on her husband to intervene with her Salvadoran caregiver:

> I would say to her, I don't want the kids to chew gum . . . and she just didn't get it. Knowing she comes from this Hispanic background, it's kinda macho, I would just have my husband tell her. He'd come in, man of the house type of thing, [and say] "Okay, Elena, no chewing gum, never any chewing gum," and she'd go, "Okay, Mr. Burton, no problem."

In hierarchical households where husbands see the domestic sphere as their wives' responsibility, they also see securing the right caregiver, and managing her properly, as their wives' duty. Some mothers described their husbands as ordering them to fire particular caregivers who had annoyed them or who did not meet their housekeeping standards. Mothers are sometimes pained by these decisions, but some feel that they have no choice but to please their husbands.

Others are motivated to persuade dissatisfied husbands that caregivers should be retained. A Los Angeles lawyer has kept her long-term Guatemalan caregiver despite grumbling from her husband: "He gets annoyed because this isn't done or that isn't done and I have had to exert a tempering kind of influence, saying, Listen, here are the tradeoffs. I've been able to talk him out of anything drastic." A Los Angeles couple with three children had good luck with their first several caregivers. Then they went through fourteen in six months. One had a hit-and-run accident in their car, which the parents learned about when they got a summons; another told the children they would be sent to jail; a third allowed the children to spend the day making dozens of calls to the mother's work associates. "We went from one nightmare to another. Horrible." They now have a Guatemalan caregiver who is responsible, but slower-moving than they would like. The mother said she had decided to settle for her. "My husband wasn't happy about the decision. I said, 'Frank, I am so tired. This has been the worst period. . . . She's not optimal, but I want to stay with her for now.'" Parents learn realism, as well as confidence, as employers.

## EXPECTATIONS OF EMOTIONAL COMMITMENT

Most low-paid jobs involve little worker commitment. Caregiving jobs are unusual in that employers expect an emotional investment for a small salary. Parents look for caregivers who put children first and money second. Highly motivated caregivers themselves describe the work as something that should be done only by those who love children. They think many fellow workers take it up for the wrong reasons. This is not surprising, as workers who have few options do not pick jobs on the basis of personal preference. Caregivers object, though, to the suggestion that emotional rewards should substitute for economic ones.

Most employers think the trick is to find workers who naturally have loving and child-oriented natures. Some see entire ethnic or racial groups as liberally endowed with these characteristics. Many Los Angeles employers describe Latina women as loving and indulgent toward children. On the East Coast, parents see women "from the islands" (the Caribbean) as deriving pride and gratification from close relationships with children. As they become experienced employers, parents learn to make finer distinctions among candidates. They eliminate those who seem mercenary. While upwardly mobile professionals consider it a sign of self-respect to ask for high salaries and job perks, caregivers' frank inquiries about wages can be viewed with suspicion. As a Los Angeles mother said, "You become an expert at screening. The people that call up and ask how much do you pay, you just say that the position's been filled, because you know they're only shopping for dollars." New York parents of twins interviewed job candidates at length and pressed them about whether they would commit to three to five years' employment and a possible move to Connecticut. Trying to exclude money-oriented candidates, the father gathered much information from each before revealing the salary.

Parents who like their caregivers stress their "good" motives in taking jobs. A Manhattan couple, the husband a professor and the wife a social service administrator, interviewed an experienced Jamaican caregiver. At first she hesitated to take the job, which involved a substantial pay cut. The mother thought the reluctance might have stemmed from fear she would get too attached to their baby. "Louise is a very loving person and she loves my daughter to pieces." This caregiver had not emphasized her economic demands, allowing the parents to interpret her hesitation as they wished.

The parents' emphasis on the deeper gratifications of caregiving can be frustrating for caregivers, even those who believe, as the parents do, that the job transcends money. The parents' attitude can make it hard for caregivers to request raises. Many never do. They wait for parents to offer them more, and if they do not, will look for a new job rather than ask. Some who do ask can meet with irritation from their employers. An Irish nanny took a job in Manhattan where it was agreed in advance that, if she proved satisfactory, she would receive a raise after three months. At the end of the three months, she asked the mother about the raise. The mother put her off. Later that day, the mother pointedly asked the caregiver whether she had any change from a small errand. The caregiver got the message that by being so bold as to ask for her raise, some element of trust had been lost.

Parents can also be hurt if caregivers ask for money for special services. They believe that at a certain point their relationship goes beyond such considerations. A Los Angeles lawyer who has had a Guatemalan caregiver for eight years has been surprised that when the caregiver works extra hours or days, she asks for extra pay. The mother said, "We really thought we had developed more of a personal relationship, and things shouldn't be on a dollar basis."

Parents' expectations regarding caregiver loyalty and commitment are most evident when caregivers announce they are leaving. Some employers take it personally and reproach the caregivers, not all of whom are sympathetic. When an Irish caregiver, dismayed at being in the wilds of New Jersey, told her employers she was leaving for Manhattan, the mother "was angry at me. And I was like, well, that's the way the cookie crumbles. I can't stay here just because you're upset." This mother later refused to write a reference for the caregiver. An English nanny said the father who employed her would not look at her for a week after she gave notice. Caregivers know departures can become tense. This is one reason short-term caregivers leave without announcing the fact. Fifteen of the seventy-nine employers interviewed reported that they had caregivers who had left without notice.

## CAREGIVERS' DEMANDS ON PARENTS

Parents' problems in managing domestic workers arise in part from lack of experience. They also reflect a basic dilemma over the limits of the caregiving relationship. They ask more from the caregiver than would be expected in ordinary business relations, but they are not sure they want to transcend their own roles as employers. Some workers never turn to their employers for help with their personal problems, but many do. Most class peers who work as caregivers do not have dependents and almost never ask for emergency money. Their own families usually provide them with financial and emotional support if crises arise. Class subordinates, far from having families that can help them, usually support dependents. Their children may become sick; they themselves may need medical or dental care; or they can be harassed by landlords. Those who are in the country illegally do not have access to government services.

Those parents who employ a series of low-wage workers in rapid succession tend not to get entangled in their lives. Employers with caregivers they value and want to retain face more difficult decisions. They describe being approached by immigrant caregivers for many different types of assistance, but most commonly for loans. Caregivers engage in forced saving by borrowing the money first and then paying it back via salary deductions. Latina caregivers mainly do this so they can bring children or other relatives to the United States. Some employers also pay medical and dental bills, sometimes taking caregivers to their own doctors. They use their professional expertise to help caregivers deal with landlords and creditors. Employers who were lawyers helped caregivers get relatives out of jail, and one took legal action against her caregiver's bigamous husband. One Los Angeles couple helped arrange their Guatemalan caregiver's wedding and lent her fiancé a suit for the occasion.

Some employers do not mind these requests. One, herself from the Dominican Republic, said it would never cross her mind to ask her caregiver the purpose of a loan; she automatically writes a check. Another Los Angeles employer cried when discussing her Mexican caregiver's hardships; the caregiver was almost the sole support of her widowed mother and four siblings. This employer said, "I feel that somehow we are supporting them and that makes things more personal." A Manhattan mother, a lawyer, found that her proud and reserved caregiver, an older woman from Trinidad, had breast cancer. The caregiver had always been a day worker, but the mother prevailed on her to recuperate from surgery for six weeks in the employer's apartment.

Other employers quickly tire of requests for aid. They cut off caregivers they consider too problem-ridden or demanding. One Los Angeles mother said her Salvadoran caregiver took advantage of them: "She was only with us for four months, and in that four-month period she managed to borrow money to the amount of $600, and she had a color television that she took home so that her kids could use it." Despite feeling they had "a lot to share," the mother said that, looking back, she felt resentful.

Employers tend to be more resentful when class subordinates take time than when they take money. They hire caregivers to reduce their load and become angry when they add to it. When the Salvadoran caregiver of Los Angeles employers became pregnant, the mother served her dinner in her room because she got easily tired. But the mother got irritated: "She was just taking advantage of the fact that I would do it. There's just certain types of people, if there's an inch, they'll take it." Another Los Angeles mother said she drove all over town to help her Salvadoran employee get immigration documents, but did not think the caregiver showed sufficient gratitude.

Even the most loyal employers, who care deeply about their employees, do not forget that in offering aid they are also cementing ties that can help their children. The mother who nursed the caregiver for six weeks said it was a natural thing to do, given her personal relationship with the caregiver and her values. Plus, she added, "you don't ever want to piss anybody off, because they're taking care of your children."

# DISTRUST OF CLASS
# SUBORDINATES' WORLD

Employers may offer caregivers a small slice of their resources, but most do not want to be drawn into their socially subordinate caregivers' world. Most employers strive for social distance and can be particularly negative about having the boyfriends or husbands of caregivers come to their homes. This can reflect class and ethnic bias, but in some instances derives from caregivers' statements about abusive men in their lives. A Manhattan employer went to work late many mornings because she listened to her distraught Puerto Rican caregiver complain about her abusive husband, with whom she alternately fought and reconciled. The employer's patience ended when she learned the husband, who carried a gun, had been at her own apartment. A Los Angeles employer fired a caregiver who told her that she had become involved with a man she met on a bus; the man, she explained, was a convicted child molester who had to keep a specified distance from places with children. Even when parents know nothing negative about caregivers' boyfriends, they generally are not eager to have them visit.

When discussing employees who were class peers, no parents who were interviewed expressed fear of their boyfriends. They see these men as part of a world they know. The most negative comment about an au pair's relationship came from parents who were alarmed when she took up with a succession of working-class African-American men, one of whom she married. This Belgian au pair abandoned the "safety" of men of her own class and race, arousing the type of anxiety in the parents that more often occurs with caregivers who are class subordinates.

Parents also fear theft more often from class subordinates than class peers. No employers we interviewed experienced any thefts by class peers or by long-term workers who were class subordinates. A half-dozen parents, though, said that short-term class-subordinate caregivers had stolen from them. Some saw it almost as a cost of having employees. In one case, the situation went beyond pilferage. A seventeen-year-old Colombian caregiver in Los Angeles stole cameras, jewelry, and silverware from neighbors up and down the employer's block. Alerted by a neighbor, police took the caregiver away in handcuffs. The parents felt pity for her, which intensified when they learned she had tried to commit suicide while in jail. The parents responded to the trauma by switching to hiring college students.

Socially subordinate caregivers often fear being falsely accused of theft.[2] Two Latina caregivers reported their employers sometimes searched their purses. On a more subtle level, Marta, a Mexican immigrant, detects a note of distrust in her employer's questions about her possessions. Marta said:

> She is always forgetting where she's left her belongings and then says things like "I left this, that, or the other thing here." I feel bad because what if she thinks since I'm the one who cleaned that I stole it or something. So then I say, "No, I didn't see it" and then inevitably she finds it somewhere else and says, "I'm sorry, I'm sorry." But I don't respond.

A Los Angeles mother, a lawyer married to a lawyer, gets along well with her Filipina caregiver, but the mother is surprised by the caregiver's fear of being accused of stealing.

> She is very paranoid about being accused of theft. She's very devout and so I'm probably certain that she doesn't steal. But she's from a very poor family. And she's very sensitive. I've never accused her. And I have no reason to. And it'll be silly things like I can't find Sara's black skirt and she'll say, "Well, I didn't take it."

Similarly, a caregiver from Trinidad says she has always refused to work with another employee. "Somewhere along the line, one might be mistrusted. Things might be missing and then there is a problem. So I prefer to do child care and housework by myself." Socially subordinate caregivers have few resources to defend themselves against employer accusations.

The distrust that can lurk beneath the surface of caregiving arrangements can be seen in some parents' fear of reprisals when they have conflicts with caregivers. Such anxieties are not common, but it is revealing that they appear at all. Seven employers who hired and then fired class subordinates said the conflicts made them fear their caregivers would seek revenge. Two of these employers changed their locks, and the other five tried to ease the final parting to diminish the chances of retribution. One woman, who had dismissed her Guatemalan caregiver, was initially angered when her husband, arriving home as the woman was leaving, hugged her and thanked her for all she had done. On reflection, she thought maybe it was a good thing: "I didn't trust Juanita a hundred percent, and I felt that maybe it was better if she went thinking one of us was okay, so that she wouldn't seek some sort of revenge."

One Los Angeles doctor explained that her husband made sure he could track down caregivers in case they disappeared with the baby:

> That's something that my husband instituted right off the bat with these housekeepers. We have a video camera, and during their first couple of weeks, we take pictures of them with the baby. We always offer to drive them home the first couple of weeks so we know exactly where they live. The two housekeepers that didn't come back, they could have taken our child and we'd never know where to find them in the barrio.

The mother added that she herself was not so concerned, but that her husband's family had suffered from Nazi violence and retained a certain insecurity. A New York couple asked Caribbean job candidates to detail their siblings' occupations;

the employers said they worried that relatives who had been in Attica might someday show up on their doorstep. In a society where class and race segregation usually keep people in homogeneous worlds, personal encounters across lines of race and class can be fraught with fears that surpass rational anxieties. These types of fears are never expressed about class peers.[3]

## THE NEEDS OF CLASS PEERS

The relationships between parents and class-peer caregivers often go beyond normal employment boundaries, as discussed in chapter 3. Some parents try to incorporate these workers into their families, a process made easier because of the temporary nature of the relationship. Beyond extending general family goodwill to such caregivers, parents may also have to intervene in their emotional problems.

While fear of theft and a vague sense of menace or unease can tinge parents' relationships with some class subordinates, unease about possible emotional breakdowns is more common with class peers. Many class peers are young and are away from home for the first time. They are not work-hardened veterans, determined to endure so that they can support their own children. These are young women who want to combine adventure, travel, and child care. Some find their new situations more demanding than they expected. In addition, some class peers who take up child care are emotionally troubled, downwardly mobile people who do not cope well in the homes of privileged, successful employers.

A number of employers we interviewed reported experiences with troubled caregivers from middle-class backgrounds. One Los Angeles couple, both psychologists, who hired a German au pair found her the third night on the job sitting on the floor in the hall, completely disoriented. The mother concluded the au pair was having a psychotic episode. She got her back into bed, and then lay awake all night wondering "What the hell is going on here? Who is this person?" The mother found out the next day that the family who had recommended her knew she was seriously troubled and had decided she could not care for *their* children. The new employer did a "therapeutic intervention" and persuaded the au pair to go back to Germany. Other employers interviewed had middle-class American caregivers they described as "basket cases," "truly weird," or "very strange" people.

While full-blown breakdowns are rare, class peers who stay in caregiving jobs for years can suffer serious problems of self-esteem. Sheltered and isolated, they can lose the capacity to manage independently. A forty-year-old Irish nanny has an easy job with powerful Manhattan employers. Used to living in luxury, she hates the subway and fears the only neighborhoods where she could afford her own apartment. An English nanny commented that she is fifty years old and has no home or family of her own. When depressed women share families' lives, parents can find they have acquired emotional dependents. Depression not only takes a heavy toll on the women themselves, but has implications for the kind of care they can offer.[4]

Occasionally employers can help caregivers who have lost their self-confidence. An American college graduate who worked for a Los Angeles family for five years was so embarrassed to be a caregiver that she lied to her family about her work. Her employer tried to buck her up, calling her "my infant development specialist," but the caregiver viewed herself as a "nothing." In her case, the employers had class resources that proved of value. The mother encouraged her to apply to graduate school, helped her fill out applications, and ultimately supervised her dissertation. Without this very practical and special aid, the caregiver believes she would have continued to see herself as "basically useless." Most other long-term employees who are class peers are not so lucky; the parents who hire them find it more convenient to ignore the emotional problems the caregiving job creates or intensifies.

## UNSUPERVISED WORKERS,
## NEGLECTED CHILDREN

Parents can worry about caregivers' honesty or emotional state, but these are trivial concerns compared to parents' deeper fears of their children coming to harm. No cases of abuse were turned up in these interviews, although some marginal situations of harsh treatment were reported.[5] There were, however, three cases of serious neglect of babies. In two of the cases, the caregiver was a class subordinate, and in one a class peer. The parents discovered they had little insight into their caregivers and less control over them.

In one case, a Manhattan doctor and her CPA husband hired a young African-American woman to look after their baby son. The mother early began sensing that the caregiver was not being forthright with her. Feeling uneasy, she and her husband took a step that gave them moral qualms: they secretly video-taped the caregiver. The two-hour tape shows the difference between display and reality in the caregiving world. The tape begins with the caregiver entering the apartment in the morning and affectionately greeting the baby. She holds the baby up to her face and speaks playfully with him. When the door closes on the mother, however, the caregiver's demeanor changes. Her smile disappears and she instantly becomes somber. She puts the baby on the floor; when he starts to cry, she takes him up and, holding him under her arm like a football, carries him into the next room, where she places him in his crib. For the rest of the tape, she never interacts with him again.

The tape captures a phone call the caregiver received from the mother. When the caregiver, who had been lying on the couch looking depressed, answers the phone, her animated expression instantly returns. She says, "Oh, I'll let the baby speak to you," and holds the phone out to a baby who in reality is in the next room. With a bright voice, the caregiver says to the mother, "Baby says hi." This caregiver had mastered the art of seeming to tend to the baby as her middle-class employers would wish.

In the second case, a New York couple, both employed in the corporate sector, hired a caregiver from St. Vincent in the West Indies to look after their one-year-old twins. The couple had done an extremely thorough job of checking applicants and at first thought they had found an excellent caregiver. Betty coped with the twins well. Her own life was harsh. She was a live-in employee during the week; her seven-year-old son stayed with a relative a short distance away. The boy used to call his mother at night, until the repeated calls annoyed the employers; the caregiver promised that they would end once she had saved enough to buy a TV for the boy (as proved to be the case). Gradually other problems emerged, including Betty's frequent requests for extra money. The mother usually obliged, hoping it would inspire Betty to provide good care. The parents' doubts about Betty increased when a neighbor said he had seen Betty invite a man into their apartment. The employers set up a hidden video camera. The mother described herself as hysterical when she watched it. The eight-hour tape shows Betty almost entirely ignoring the twins. She kept them in their cribs in another room, while she watched TV.

The third case was similar in outline. A New Jersey doctor/lawyer couple employed a young French woman to care for their infant son. The doctor mother came home unexpectedly in the middle of the day and found her baby still in his crib, lying awake in urine-soaked pajamas. The cleaning woman told her the au pair often left the baby in his crib for most of the day.

The mother of the twins said she "was in very bad shape for a long time" after watching the tape. She went into therapy to help her deal with the knowledge that for half a year her twins had been left to scream in their cribs for hours. The French au pair's employers were shocked that for months they had shared their lives with a charming young woman who had no concern for their baby.

The two families that employed class subordinates fired them. In each case, though, they gave a false reason for the dismissal, not wanting to alert the caregivers to the taping or to antagonize them. Both families gave the fired caregivers generous severance pay to avoid possible reprisals. The au pair was not fired. The community representative of the agency that had recruited her helped work out a resolution; this was made easier because the au pair was scheduled to depart in two months. The parents agreed she could stay if she promised to reform. They gave her Penelope Leach's *Your Baby and Child* to read. Chastened, the au pair looked after the baby conscientiously.

The mother of the twins and the Manhattan doctor both considered quitting work. Instead, they changed their hiring strategies. The doctor switched to class peers, hiring college students. The mother of the twins wanted to move in the same direction. She said, "I had decided that part of the problem was cultural. I wanted someone that thinks more like I do, that's more like me." She hired a young Israeli, but found the twins were too demanding for anyone but an experienced woman. She now has a caregiver from Trinidad, but she has become a tougher employer. She attributed the original debacle to her laxness: "It was entirely my fault because I gave in to her too much. I felt that she was ruling me rather than me ruling her and I don't want to be in that situation again."

Each of these situations involved alert, child-oriented parents. They proved unable to predict the performance of the caregivers they hired. When with the parents, each caregiver came across as involved and committed. Caregivers in the New York area were asked in interviews whether they thought such situations occurred very often. They would not say often, but they did say that the occupation permitted a certain level of deception. Parents may attribute caregiver failure to their own lax management, but any control strategies will be ultimately ineffective in the area where they matter most, the care children receive when the parents aren't at home. In reality, most caregivers are unsupervised most of the time, and parents' struggles for control can involve peripheral issues as much as core ones. Although the great majority of caregivers act responsibly, the privacy of the middle-class home can create risks in private care.[6]

This in fact is the conclusion reached by one mother. Sandra Scarr, a psychologist and child care expert, hired a practical nurse to look after her eighteen-month-old daughter. When she returned home one afternoon, the child cried, "Kathy hit me, Kathy hit me." The caregiver ran out the door. Scarr found her daughter had been beaten and she called the police; they told her the woman had beaten other children before, but there had never been sufficient evidence to convict her. Although Scarr had relied on caregivers to look after her two older children as well, the experience led her to rethink her child care choice when it came to her fourth child.

> I am not opposed in principle to babysitters in one's home. I have had a couple of good ones, more mediocre ones, and the one disaster. The lack of supervision and public examination of what can go on in the home is a major problem, in my view—one which led me to send my last child to a day care home.[7]

## CONCLUSIONS

Parents can benefit from their caregivers' labor only if they can control it. This requires thought, effort, and a certain ruthlessness. Most learn to manage their employees, but not all parents find they are suited to this role. Some shrink from confronting employees, telling them what to do, or correcting their mistakes. Ideologically or personally, they are not comfortable with the master–servant relationship.

Few parents, however, can afford to be passive. Given the stakes—the care and socialization of their children—they strive, with varying levels of success and tension, to get caregivers to act as they wish. They have the power to hire and to fire. To succeed as employers, they must confront and cope with individual personalities, a force neutralized in bureaucracies but powerfully operative in households, and one that to a degree can overcome even class advantage.

Even the most skilled and tenacious employers, however, cannot really control what is most important to them, the caregivers' treatment of their children when they are alone together. Employers can engage in many skirmishes on side issues, but cannot count on having their wishes respected when they are not home to make it happen. Once children can talk, they become independent sources of information and the problem lessens. With preverbal children, however, parents' control of domestic workers rests uncertainly on faith and intuition.

# CHAPTER 5

# Clashes in Values

Despite frequent differences in background, caregivers and parents see each other so intimately and depend on each other so greatly that they become aware of each other's ways of thinking. This throws their own value systems into relief. They come to realize how differently people can approach child rearing, leading a few to reconsider their own values and most to reaffirm them.

Caregivers walk a fine line; if they suppress their own values too completely they can partially lose their creativity and judgment, qualities that make adults good guides for children. They also know, though, that they are not the final decision makers. All adults who look after other people's children face similar dilemmas.[1] Those who work in child care centers, however, usually have some type of training that gives them systematic exposure to child-rearing ideologies and approaches that may differ from their own. Researchers have found that this training does make a difference in how caregivers respond to children. "With more training in child development, daycare providers are more knowledgeable, and they are also more interactive, helpful, talkative, playful, positive, and affectionate with the children in their care."[2] In essence, courses in child development help socialize caregivers into a broadly "middle class" type of care, where engagement with the child is crucial. In private homes, value differences tend to emerge piecemeal, with many possibilities for misunderstanding and confusion. They also become tangled in issues of power and control.

Caregivers, not presented with an alternative ideology in any systematic or compelling way, can be mystified, as well as troubled, by what they observe in middle-class homes. For their part, most parents do not understand their caregivers' value systems in any depth. Some au pairs argue with parents about how children should be treated; most socially subordinate caregivers do not. Parents and caregivers may not talk to each other often, or may only discuss practical matters. Many parents, though, observe concrete differences in how they and their employees treat children. Ironically, as with issues of control, it is the parents with the most egalitarian ideologies who can end up the most conflicted. They have competing principles: They want to respect their caregivers' judgments and ideas, yet they want their children treated according to their own beliefs about what is developmentally sound.

Parents may think that encouraging children to know what they want and to feel free to ask for it will make them self-motivated, confident, and articulate as adults. But caregivers may see these children as intolerably demanding. One Salvadoran employee expressed wonderment and disgust that the little girl she took care of used as many as four different cups when she had tea, trying to decide which color she preferred. The father supplied her with new ones as her preferences changed. To the caregiver, this was indulgence run amok. For the father, it may have been a way of avoiding protest, but also it may have reflected a deeper feeling that the girl's tastes were legitimate (even if unstable). Middle-class American parents, used to jobs where they operate with some authority and independence, encourage young children early on to develop their own tastes and opinions.[3]

Few middle-class parents are interested in structured academic learning for preschool children.[4] They do not want flash cards, but they want their children to be in rich environments where they learn naturally and informally. Since the mid-1960s, the child-rearing ante has been raised. Parents' anxieties have been increased by experts' emphasis on the early development of cognitive skills.[5] Combined with worry that professional jobs are increasingly hard to get, parents fear that their children will not compete successfully with others. In cities such as New York and Los Angeles, parents struggle to get their children into elite preschools that can pave the way to exclusive private schools. From early on, children face cold-eyed scrutiny from school directors, who can pick and choose freely among applicants.[6] Some parents keep their children out of school for a year if they have summer or fall birthdays, wanting them to have an edge over younger classmates. Beneath a seemingly relaxed child-rearing style, middle-class parents hope to prepare children emotionally and intellectually for the decades of schooling that lie ahead of them.[7]

Immigrant caregivers—usually raised in harsher worlds than the children in their charge, where disciplined effort to help their families counted for more than academic success—may disagree with their employers' child-rearing methods as a matter of principle. Beyond this, the indulging of children has direct costs for them. It is more work to take care of children whose opinions must be consulted. In homes where parents do not try to rein in their children, caregivers can also take the brunt of children's unrestrained temper. In the worst situations, caregivers can become deeply indignant at what they experience. Not able to take a strong stand, or to express their own values, they may withdraw. In other homes, caregivers can face a more complex conflict of values; they can come to see some benefits of their employers' child-rearing styles, while not fully embracing them.

Most dual-career middle-class parents believe they themselves provide a good learning environment when they are with their children in the evenings and on weekends, but may have doubts about whether their children's caregivers provide it. This leads some to a seemingly simple solution: hiring class peers. As we have seen, though, this choice involves its own complications. Others hire class subordinates but develop a range of strategies to try to make sure their children are socialized as they wish, despite likely differences in background and values. This chapter examines value differences and parents' strategies for dealing with them.

## WHAT IMMIGRANT CAREGIVERS THINK ABOUT AMERICAN CHILDREN

With some exceptions, the Latina and Caribbean caregivers in this study came from rural and working-class backgrounds. Most came from large families. The Latina caregivers interviewed averaged six siblings; the Caribbean caregivers averaged seven. They had had limited opportunity for education. Most commonly, the caregivers' schooling stopped at the elementary level. These women typically have major economic burdens, supporting not only themselves but elderly parents and their own children, or sometimes younger brothers and sisters. They begin work early in life and most expect to continue until they are old, as they do not have pensions or Social Security.

When they first start working in American households, Third World caregivers are often surprised by the way their employers raise their children. Of course, caregivers talk among themselves and try to prepare newcomers for what they will find. They describe American child-rearing patterns and warn women new to the work that in America parents treat their children very delicately. Despite advance preparation, some caregivers can still can be startled by what they see as a faulty balance of power. The children strike them as unduly indulged. Caregiver after caregiver mentioned this phenomenon, most contrasting it unfavorably with the adult-run homes they came from. A thirty-year-old Mexican caregiver in Los Angeles said that in the United States, "parents spoil their children. That is why they are stubborn and bad-mannered. Their parents don't teach them to be respectful. They say horrible things. Sometimes the bigger boy tells me that I'm an idiot. What can I do? If he were my boy I'd slap him so that he could respect me." The mother, she says, does not object when the boy insults her. "She always tells them that they can express whatever they feel, that she knows they're angry and that's why they're saying those things."

Some caregivers described the children they deal with as stubborn and rude. A twenty-year-old Mexican woman found the five-year-old girl she cared for "incredibly intolerable." The girl would ask her to get things, and then would add, "Hurry up!" The caregiver yearned for a Mexican-style household.

> In Mexico, we are raised differently. The parents will tell us "This is not right" and one has to obey. Here it is very different. The little girls will say, "I want to do this" and if the parents say, "It's not a good idea," the children will get upset and create a fuss until they can do what they want.

Others also commented that American children could usually get what they wanted. A twenty-year-old Salvadoran caregiver said, "Latino children, if they want something, they rarely get it. Even if they cry and cry they rarely get it. Whereas [North American children] get whatever they want." Caregivers think the parents themselves cannot control their children well, so as mere employees they have no chance of doing so. As one Guatemalan caregiver put it, "Imagine us, who are not even their mothers" trying to assert control.

Overall, the Latina caregivers who were interviewed were more negative about American child-rearing patterns than the Caribbeans were. This may stem from the greater powerlessness of Latina women, as many speak little or no English and cannot participate in the more subtle aspects of child rearing.

The Caribbean women operated as if they had more authority and this made them less vulnerable to children's abuse. They might disagree in principle with American child-rearing attitudes, but had less reason to feel victimized.

Caregivers were often angered by seeing children sitting idle, while they themselves were hard at work. Raised to help their parents at an early stage, these women were surprised that American children, by and large, had no responsibilities except to do their schoolwork. The parents, said a Mexican caregiver, let their children be lazy, because they had servants to pick up after them. "Here the kids just play and go to school."

Differences in child-rearing style are not abstract matters for employees, but practical concerns, as they affect the caregivers' own authority. The more power children have, the more cautious caregivers have to be about crossing them. As a Guatemalan woman put it, "I have gotten used to this way because it is my job and I have to accustom myself to it." Caregivers don't want children to complain to their parents about them. Another Guatemalan woman, with a fourth-grade education (and six children of her own), said of the six-year-old boy in her charge, "I don't try to stop him from doing things, because that's the way his parents are. Whatever he wants to do is okay with me." Otherwise, "he could turn against me." Caregivers worried about having to win children over, because children's attachment to them provided their best job security.

## VALUE DIFFERENCES BETWEEN PARENTS AND CAREGIVERS

The caregivers note their employers' emphasis on education. They comment that North Americans spend a lot of time reading to their children, which did not usually happen in their own households. Caregivers also observe that children's main duty is to do well in school. They see parents as encouraging children to talk and to learn to express themselves. A Guatemalan caregiver noted her employers' style of conversation: "They include their children in their conversations and we don't do that. When adults [in Guatemala] are communicating, it is just with adults, not with children."

Caregivers with little formal schooling tend to emphasize children's moral rather than intellectual development. When Latina caregivers say they would like to be able to "educate" the children in their charge, they mean they would like to teach them right from wrong.

Not all class subordinates remain hostile to the parents' child-rearing style. Some take a step out of their own culture and like some of what they see. Santos, a forty-three-year-old Mexican caregiver with four children of her own, was impressed by the way her employers created a structured environment for their three children.

> We let our children watch whatever they want on TV; [the employers] don't. We let them eat candy and not take naps; they don't. They buy their children lots of instructive toys. When my kids were little, I didn't do this. I would buy them the toys that they wanted. From the moment the child can see, can think, can move, the parents buy instructive toys. If I were to become a mother all over again, I would buy these instructive toys.

Another Mexican woman went further, saying that her American employers do better by their children than most parents do in her own culture. Forty-nine years old, also with four children of her own, she likes her employers and has come to appreciate the way they raise their children. Latino parents, she said, do not allow children to

> freely be themselves. We hold them back; it is as if we tie them up with a rope. Here they let their children bloom, their will, their artistic talents or whatever. This is really good because you are forming an individual who will have

broad capacities. [In Mexico] you couldn't even express yourself because your mother and father would silence you.

The woman added that it was more work bringing up children the North American way. To allow children to develop properly, adults had to see what they were trying to do and remove obstacles, so that they could manage on their own. "This is very tiring because you constantly have to keep your eyes open."

A thirty-one-year-old Guatemalan caregiver in Los Angeles, who left school when she was thirteen, was impressed by her employer's patience in dealing with her young son. "I think that they perhaps raise their children in a better way because [when the child is misbehaving] she talks to him even if he doesn't listen." Money, she thought, might make the difference: the mother did not have to demand anything of the child—any contribution to the household, or early independence—because nothing was needed from him.

The caregivers who admired their employers' style of child rearing did not always think it would be practical in their own culture. Because dealing with children who had their own ideas and who wanted to join adult conversations took work and patience, it helped if parents were not tired and did not have many competing demands. Santos thought the mother she worked for was remarkably patient; she ignored small acts of misbehavior that Santos said would have agitated her. She thought perhaps the parents could pursue their tolerant, attentive child-rearing style because they were "never tired." They did no physical work, so they did not get exhausted as did many of the men (laborers) and women (housecleaners) in Santos's world. The parents "go home to a clean house, their children are already attended to and cared for, because they have the means to pay someone else to do it." For her own part, she had to work at the employers' house, and then go home and start with her own four children, cleaning house and supervising them.

One gets home and it's like the day is starting over again, attend the family, do the wash, shopping. This is the way it is for those who don't have money to pay [someone else]. So they [the employers] can ignore things that one can't ignore, because you expect that your own children will help you with the work. They don't demand that the children help them. They don't get home and get upset and start fighting with the children about the mess because they will pay for someone to clean it up.

Parents hope for loving warmth from caregivers. They may not understand the caregivers' attitudes may be more complex than it appears on the surface. Sometimes employers find it illuminating to see how caregivers treat their own children. One Los Angeles mother was surprised that her Guatemalan caregiver, Lydia, who was highly attentive to the employers' children, did not actually believe this was either necessary or desirable. When Lydia's alcoholic husband assaulted her, the employers invited her and her baby to live with them. The mother noticed that Lydia did not share her belief that babies should be held when fed.

I'm amazed how little she holds him to feed him. She's quite happy to just prop up a bottle and let him feed himself, and that has alarmed me. I told her that when she needs to feed him it's quite all right if she sits down and hugs him, but she tells me that this is how it's done in Guatemala. She wouldn't hold her children. She has four children back in Guatemala and she apparently would never hold them. There are too many things to do and her attitude was that "if I hold him he gets used to it, and over time he expects it, some day I may not be able to do it, so why train him that way?"

The mother realized she could not count on Lydia to share her beliefs. Lydia had come from a very different world, where to raise a "high-demand" child was to create expectations that probably could not be consistently met. Lydia's employers, however, paid her to meet *their* expectations regarding their children's care, and Lydia struggled to do this. She said that she watched the parents closely to see how they treated their children, and she then tried to treat them the same way. She retained strong reservations, even if she did not express them to the parents. She felt that because the parents let the children do as they chose, the children came to believe they ruled the roost. Lydia said Latinos raised their children differently. "I have gotten used to this way because it is my job and I have to accustom myself to it. But with my own children, I do it differently." Lydia worried that as the children got older, they would become still more demanding toward her.

Watching their caregivers, parents often observe that they play differently with the children than they themselves do. Sometimes the undercurrent running through the parents' comments is the idea that the caregivers are not very bright. Parents tend to see them as being satisfied with boring activities. Here, as in other realms, parents can quite easily slide into denigration of the women they hire. A New Jersey doctor commented with some wonderment that her caregiver was willing to draw hundreds of Barbie dolls; a real estate lawyer with a Jamaican caregiver said she was not bright, "but if you were very bright, you could not do this job without going crazy." Parents sometimes describe caregivers as participating in activities on the children's level. A mother of two daughters, who does freelance desktop publishing, noted that her caregiver, from Kenya, did not play with her three-year-old daughter as she herself did:

> We've got these alphabet blocks and I told her that when Linda plays with the alphabet blocks she could point out what the letters are and what the sound is that the letter makes. She plays a lot differently with them than I do. Her style of play is a lot less as teacher than just as a playmate, just keeping them entertained. With me, I'm wanting them to get something out of every experience.

Parents take a long-range view of children's development, but they hire employees of uncertain job tenure, who almost certainly will take a shorter-range view. Employers worry that caregivers do what is easiest at the moment, whether this involves feeding the children junk-food snacks or letting them watch TV. One Los Angeles mother said that in her experience, caregivers gave the children whatever they wanted: "It's like, Well, let 'em have it; it's like they don't want to be bothered." Some employers see this attitude as intrinsic to caregivers' outlooks. There are, however, structural reasons for caregivers and parents to have different time orientations. Most caregivers do not get to see the children in their charge grow up; whatever investment they make, they are denied the experience of its fruition. Although many long-term caregivers come to love the children in their charge, caregivers who move from job to job say they learn not to let themselves get too attached the way novice workers and the unsophisticated do.

The different backgrounds and hierarchical positions of parents and caregivers make value divergence likely. Employers develop a range of strategies for dealing with this divergence. They try to directly and indirectly control caregivers' treatment of their children; they initiate educational activities with their children and enroll them in preschools run by trained professionals, and they replace class subordinates with class peers as children become verbal and, in the parents' eyes, more intellectually demanding. Caregivers represent only one part of a complex socialization strategy. They play key roles for a period, but their employers limit or change those roles as they see fit.

## DIRECT AND INDIRECT EFFORTS TO CONTROL CAREGIVERS' PERFORMANCE

Nearly all parents who employ caregivers maintain control over crucial areas of child rearing. In these areas, they simply tell caregivers how they want them to operate, although sometimes they do not do so until they become aware of problems. The four main areas where parents set rules are discipline, safety, health, and nutrition. Even the most tentative employers usually feel strongly about these matters and believe they have the right to demand that their wishes be followed. Caregivers usually understand that they will be fired if they do not implement parents' decisions in these areas. Parents do not want their children to come to harm, a goal even more central than having their children learn and enjoy themselves, but one that also has its culturally specific elements.

In the area of discipline, nearly all parents tell caregivers not to hit their children. Some caregivers complained about this restriction in interviews, but they knew what was expected of them, partly because it is a matter they discuss among themselves. One Latina caregiver said that she understood it was illegal to hit children in America. A few said in interviews that they had hit children anyway, but they generally refrained from doing so.

Some parents find out their caregivers have treated their children more harshly than they would have liked. One Los Angeles mother discovered, during a conflict between two employees, that one of them had locked her eighteen-month-old, who was afraid of dogs, in a dark garage with a dog. The mother confronted her, and she did not deny the charge.

> She said that she felt that I needed help with disciplining my children. We discussed it and I told her that I never wanted that to happen again and she said that it wouldn't. But it changed my feelings towards her because I never thought that she would do anything like that. And I die if I think about it. I had trusted this woman implicitly with my children, and having heard that and knowing that had happened, I could never really trust her again.

The mother, who had thought the caregiver shared her child-rearing values, began thinking about other cultural differences that disturbed her. The caregiver shamed the older boy, a five-year-old, when he cried, telling him that only girls cried. "It was a cultural thing, and she would never, ever change that." Because of the value differences, and challenges to her authority, the mother ultimately fired the caregiver.

Another Los Angeles mother, from Westwood, found out from her Bolivian caregiver's previous employers that she had put their son in a cold shower and had washed his mouth out with soap. The new employer thought the knowledge gave her an advantage.

> From the very beginning I explained to Miranda that it's very important that she only discipline in the particular way that I allowed, which was time out, and that nothing else was allowed. No washing the mouth out with soap, no cold showers, nothing like that. I knew she was capable of doing it.

This employer, a clinical psychologist, had enough confidence in her authority and insight that she kept the caregiver, who worked for her for seven years.

Caregivers also know that they risk being fired if safety rules are not followed. In 1989, employer anxiety soared in Los Angeles, after a Latina caregiver tried to help children get to sleep by shading a lamp with a towel, which then caught fire. The caregiver escaped, but the parents returned home to find their three children dead.[8] In the wake of this tragedy, one employer we interviewed asked her Latina caregiver how she would get the children out in the event of a fire. When the caregiver answered inadequately, the employer told her to leave. Other employers fired caregivers for letting in service workers such as a cable TV installer, without their permission. A Manhattan employer fired her caregiver for twice leaving the seven-month-old baby unattended in the bath when the mother called on the phone. (Remarkably, the caregiver told the mother both times what she had done, perhaps confirming the mother's judgment that she was not sharp.) Some employers and employees share a high level of anxiety. A Los Angeles employer was delighted that her Salvadoran caregiver chose, on her own initiative, to take different routes to the market so that she would not be followed.

Rules regarding health and nutrition tend to cause more conflict between parents and caregivers, as science-based and folk traditions mesh poorly and caregivers do not entirely accept parents' authority in these areas. Parents tolerate some caregivers' ideas as harmless eccentricities. One mother was surprised to find a cabbage leaf in her child's diaper, put there by the caregiver to ward off diaper rash. The doctors among the employers interviewed have more trouble with caregivers' theories and remedies. Those wedded to the germ theory of colds see caregivers' insistence on dressing children warmly as unnecessary. Employers usually accept procedures they do not see as actively harmful, but they decisively reject any attempts to interfere with Western medical practice.

Even some employers who initially tolerate caregivers' ideas on health can become disturbed over time. A Manhattan mother, who has taken time out from her film production job, employs a seventy-five-year-old Ukrainian caregiver to help with her two boys, aged eleven and two. The caregiver, who has been employed by the family for ten years, is deeply devoted to the children, loving them, she says, as if they were her own. As part of supplying loving care, she advises the mother on remedies for common ailments. At first the mother thought that Alice exhibited folk wisdom; now she thinks she exhibits folk ignorance. Alice urged the mother to catch a frog and apply it to a wart on the older boy's toe. Alice also recommended that a foot fungus be treated by having the child step in a cow patty, an item equally difficult to obtain in Manhattan. A third incident disturbed the mother more because it brought home to her the depth of her differences with Alice. When her two-year-old started crying, Alice told her he had been given the evil eye by a stranger on the street who was jealous of his beauty. This, she said, could be cured by spitting on the child three times. More prosaically, the mother attributed the child's tears to her having turned off the TV. The mother appreciates Alice's devotion toward her sons, but she also worries about the worldview they are being exposed to.

Not all parents try to control their children's nutrition, but many do. They do not want their children fed junk food. A thirty-three-year-old Salvadoran, Margarita, working in Los Angeles, expressed her surprise over her employers' dietary requirements for their eighteen-month-old son. "I feed my children everything, but he doesn't eat salt. I am not allowed to give him fat. No candies, no cookies, no nothing. I had never heard of this in all my life, but you must do as they say." Caregivers, for their part, are often dismayed by the food available for their employers' families and for themselves while they're at work. Caregivers commonly spend their own money to buy food that they like, at least when they first come to the United States. The prevalence of prepared foods and canned items surprises them. They also dislike the lack of seasonings. As they become acclimated, though, some can adapt to a very unhealthy version of American food, which parents then try to keep away from their children. A mother described herself as perplexed by her Kenyan caregiver's feeding her children Cheese Nips and Froot Loops for lunch, given that the caregiver had worked for another American family for two years. The mother concluded that the woman's previous employers had given her specific instructions about what and what not to feed their children, a practice she then adopted.

Parents also try to enforce basic decisions about how to handle children's toilet training and sexuality. Here they do not always succeed. Some caregivers who come from other cultures have strong ideas on these matters. They can make it clear to parents they disapprove of children's late toilet training and blame parents for slowing the process. Parents can be dismayed by caregivers' negativism about any manifestation of children's sexuality. This issue caused conflict between several Los Angeles employers and their caregivers. In New York, a well-educated caregiver from Guyana, a former teacher with great sensitivity toward the children in her charge, maintains a traditional anxiety about children possibly engaging in any sex play. When she takes the young boys in her charge to visit friends, she insists on staying with them at all times, afraid, she says, that the friends' parents will not share her vigilance on the matter.

For the most part, parents and caregivers find ways to accommodate each other on these issues, but when each side feels strongly, it can lead to a parting of the ways. One Los Angeles mother was dismayed that her forty-eight-year-old Salvadoran caregiver, the only woman interviewed who had no formal education, told her daughters, seven and five, that if they did not wear underwear to bed, spiders would crawl into their vaginas. This was one factor that made the mother think perhaps she should switch caregivers: "I realized that it was something we could not overcome. I think she is uneducated, superstitious, and I couldn't change that." Another Salvadoran caregiver said she lost a job when she complained about a young girl's masturbating; the parents did not appreciate her complaints.

There are only a limited number of areas where parents can lay down explicit rules, because much caregiving involves spontaneous responses to children. Recognizing this, some parents try to indirectly control caregivers by controlling their schedules. They tell them to spend a certain amount of time at the park each day, hoping to limit passivity and TV watching. In sunny Los Angeles, some caregivers did spend a large part of the day at parks, up to about four hours. Parents also tell caregivers which television shows their children can watch and how often. Some parents allow their children to watch TV with them, but not with the caregiver. One mother, detailing her family's schedule, said that as soon as the caregiver arrived in the morning, the TV went off. As paid employees, caregivers are expected to maintain a steady focus on the children, and parents seek ways to ensure this.

## PARENTS' INSTRUCTION OF CAREGIVERS

Some parents undertake the ambitious task of trying to instruct caregivers in the more subtle aspects of their child-rearing styles, where rules are not relevant. These are parents who invest in a particular caregiver and place priority on stability. Instruction can occur both formally and informally.

Informally, some parents, almost always mothers, take several weeks off work when they first hire caregivers and spend the time working alongside them. (They contrast with other parents interviewed, who sometimes left their children with caregivers a half hour after they first appeared.) They show them how they want their children cared for, and many caregivers report that they do in fact watch mothers closely and try to do as they think they would. One Mexican caregiver said of her employers, "You have to learn the way *they* think." After a near-accident with the preschool boy in her charge, the caregiver tried to speak to him calmly: "I knew what [the mother] would have done and I did what she would have done." Some employers ask their own mothers to come and train new caregivers. Of course, for parents who take much time to train caregivers, their departure can be a serious blow.

Other parents go further and try to present their child-rearing ideas to caregivers more formally. One mother prepared a several-page theory of parenting for her caregiver when she first arrived, outlining her philosophy on a wide range of issues. It covered "theoretically, this is the right way and this is the wrong way. [For example], Paula is not a bad girl if her behavior is bad." The mother felt impelled to prepare this document because "I did a lot of reading and a lot of research and a lot of talking about what's the right way to parent and what's the wrong way, and I didn't want it to all be for naught because somebody comes in here and doesn't know what the hell they're doing."

Another mother, a Colombian living in New York, also read much child-rearing literature after the birth of her first child. "I took a lot of courses in child psychology, child development and nutrition. I tried to share those experiences with my husband, but I had a very poor reception." The husband, from a traditional Mideast culture, said he was a "normal person" and did not need expert advice. The mother instead shared her ideas with her caregiver, a fellow Colombian she had found after a year's search. She told the caregiver that "even though she might have had different techniques, I would like her to cooperate with me, because I really needed her support. I gave her material for reading." The mother thought it worked out well. The caregiver came from a family with little education and began with values very different from the mother's. At first the caregiver did whatever the children wanted, but the mother gradually instructed her in how to control them. "I would tell her to tell them no in a positive way." Seventeen years later, the caregiver is still employed by this mother and has a close relationship with the children, now in their late teens.

Parents with troubled or difficult children can make special efforts to instruct caregivers. When they fail to do so, caregivers can feel adrift, left with children whose problems are disturbing but not officially acknowledged in the household.[9] This lack of acknowledgment can cause serious alienation on the part of the caregiver. One Swedish au pair dealt with a five-year-old girl who cried from the moment the au pair woke her until she got to school, during which time the parents stayed in bed. The girl could not get along with other children, showed no enjoyment in activities, and both hit and insulted the au pair. The parents did tell the au pair that the girl was in therapy, but they did not offer her advice or support in handling the child. The au pair left after a few months.

Some parents try to bring their caregivers on board in dealing with children who require special attention or awareness by instructing the caregivers in distinctive, expert-derived modes of care. Two psychologists in Los Angeles had a difficult daughter, not seriously troubled, but described by the mother as "very hard to handle. She tests every limit, she is smart and manipulative and really tries your ability." The mother concluded that it took a very skilled person to deal with her. She asked her Mexican caregiver to help her implement an elaborate behavioral modification program, wherein the girl could earn stars and presents for cooperating. "You know, I'm a psychologist and I'm behavioral, and I apply that in the rearing of my children." The caregiver tried to do as the mother outlined, but with only partial success. She did not, the mother thought, fully comprehend the system. "She didn't really truly appreciate how to deliver reinforcements, and it was hard for her, because I think she felt resentful towards [the child] because she would be mean to her." The system, far removed from the caregiver's natural responses, called for creating a kind of emotional distance that the caregiver could not manage. Ultimately the mother and caregiver agreed that the caregiver should leave, as the child was too difficult for her.

Some caregivers reported receiving more successful instruction. A thirty-year-old Mexican caregiver, who worked for a widowed Los Angeles mother of two boys, considered quitting the job because the older of the two boys, then eight, hit and abused her. Five previous caregivers had left for the same reason. The caregiver was also depressed because the mother herself seemed overwhelmed by her situation and cried often. The mother told the caregiver that she knew the boy was difficult but that she really wanted her to stay.

> She recommended that we all go to see his psychologist. And it worked. The psychologist told me that when [the boy] is going to hit me, that I needed to grab him and hold him firmly, look him in the eyes, and tell him, "You are not going to hit me." He told me that I needed to *feel* that I was the boss.

Despite the caregiver's positive report, the mother said she did not think the caregiver was able to really follow the whole behavioral program worked out by the psychologist. The mother and caregiver had different interpretations of success; implementing the full program was beyond the caregiver's abilities or ambitions, but once she stopped the boy from hitting her she was at least willing to stay on the job.

Other parents also had mixed success trying to instruct caregivers in how to handle difficult children. A caregiver in her early twenties from a small Midwestern town worked for a New Jersey family with two adopted children, a boy of four and a girl of two. The boy was very aggressive and hostile. The caregiver felt sorry for him, because he would sometimes express intense self-hatred, but she also found him almost impossible to manage. The parents gave her child-rearing books to read, but she found them useless; she felt she needed a more practical kind of help than they offered. She also thought the parents themselves considered them a limited resource and said the parents conveyed regret over having adopted the children. Caregivers can see emotional problems that go beyond the power of any technique to remedy, despite lingering parental faith in the power of expert opinion.

Parents' child-rearing theories do not always work in practice. For reasons that are sometimes unclear, some children do not develop the emotional stability their parents want. In most of these cases, other children in the family develop more or less normally. Troubled children call forth the parents' resources, including their access to psychologists, their knowledge of expert opinion, and their efforts to instruct caregivers in special techniques to manage the children. The parents try to repair the situation and rescue their children, but even a vast structure of class-related advantages cannot overwhelm all the forces of individual psychology and personality. One New Jersey mother, warm and loving toward her children, an excellent employer according to her caregiver, has a nine-year-old son who is difficult and fearful and often beyond her control. While being interviewed, she got a call from his school saying that he was once again in trouble. When asked whether she advised the caregiver on how to handle the boy, she replied sadly, "I wish someone would advise me." Instruction only works when parents believe they have the answers.

## TASKS PARENTS KEEP FOR THEMSELVES

Although employees may provide many hours of daily care, many parents set aside crucial aspects of care to perform themselves. In divisions of household labor, class-subordinate caregivers do more of the routine work and the physical care, and parents specialize in talking and reading with their children. Nearly all educated parents read to their children in the evenings, an activity difficult for those caregivers who have little education or limited English skills. Parents will also help older children with homework, a task delegated to some class-peer employees but almost never to class subordinates. Many parents see caregivers as freeing them to specialize in "quality time" with their children.

One Manhattan mother, employed in the nonprofit sector, with a lawyer husband, wishes her Puerto Rican caregiver did more with her two girls, ten and seven, and watched TV less. She sees herself and her husband, though, as the primary forces in the girls' lives; in some respects, the caregiver's limitations help reinforce their role. The caregiver cannot help the older girl with her homework, and the mother comments, "As much as it's a pain, I think that if my child care person were doing it, I would feel left out of the process." By helping children themselves, parents show them that they value academic activities.

Some caregivers commented in interviews that parents pressure their children. A Midwestern caregiver working in New Jersey noted that where she grew up, her parents told her to do *her* best, but that in the family she works for, the goal is to be *the* best. The children strike her as very bright, but also as competitive and anxious. An Irish nanny reported that her employer was worried about his daughter in kindergarten. "Oh my gosh," he told her, "Denise has caught up on Jennifer; she can read and Jennifer can't."

Culturally specific aspects of care include not only intellectual tasks, but those connected with consumption. Parents very seldom delegate the purchase of goods to class subordinates, even when the goods involved are only groceries. Even if caregivers do most of the housework, parents keep shopping for themselves, except in rare instances (usually involving high-level immigrant employees). There are some practical reasons for this: many class subordinates cannot drive, for example. This is not the whole explanation, though, because even those who can hardly ever shop for their employers, except for picking up bread, milk, and other fill-in items.

As the parents talked about shopping in the interviews, it became evident that they viewed this as an area that required their specific skills. Their homes, usually large and well maintained, are arenas for the display of goods, and parents early teach their children about the importance of having and maintaining possessions. A "center of material display," the middle-class house is designed "not only for the private comfort of its inhabitants, but also to show visitors that the family [follows] certain canons of taste and culture."[10] Even young children are brought into this world of consumption and display through the decoration of their bedrooms and the purchase of toys for them. Caregivers marvel at the number of toys the children have. (Several commented that they felt they themselves were yet another toy.) The toys take up much space and, being composed of many small parts, require frequent organizing. Caregivers do most of this work; even those exempted from general housework, such as certain class peers, look after children's belongings. Parents can be quite demanding in this area. They insist that caregivers keep close track of these items. One Midwestern caregiver described herself as having been agitated because the two-year-old child in her charge had lost a toy truck, which the father asked her about several times. It turned out the truck was a three-dollar item. An Irish caregiver realized early on that she had to be vigilant about her five-year-old charge's toys. The mother kept a "Lost Toy Parts" list, and the caregiver dreaded seeing items going up on it.

Employers do not always trust class subordinates, in particular, to manage the family's possessions. They think caregivers do not always have the proper reverence for a family's carefully chosen goods; unaware of their distinctive quality and value, they treat them as they would ordinary objects. A Los Angeles lawyer said of her Filipina caregiver:

> Culturally, the difference is that we spend a lot of money on things with the thought that they will last a long time and they will be treasured possessions. And her background is, buy things and they're fungible. And you don't really take care of them. She cleaned a wood table with Ajax.

Even very young members of these families are heavily endowed with privately held possessions, selected by high-status people and maintained partly by low-status ones. They learn to consider their individual tastes and choices among goods to be important, just as their opinions are considered to count in other realms. Their intellectual skills, actively cultivated by their families, will, the parents hope, bring their children academic success, while their "taste" will mark them as members in good standing of a culturally privileged group.[11]

## CHILDREN'S SOCIAL LIVES

Parents can try to control or instruct their class-subordinate caregivers, but they also want their children in the company of those who share their world and culture. Both informally and formally, parents work to keep their children within middle-class circles. As children more decisively enter the world of their parents, caregivers' roles shrink from being prime socializing agents to being supporting players.

Informal socialization takes place not only in the family, but in contacts with other children and parents of similar background. Most parents try to foster their children's social lives, a task sometimes complicated by class-subordinate caregivers' exclusion from the child's social class. In middle-class culture, arranged sociability plays a large role. People make plans to see their friends rather than relying on encountering them casually. In working-class circles, meetings with friends tend to occur more on the basis of happenstance.[12] The contrast can be clearly seen in the worlds of employers and class-subordinate caregivers. The employers have the means to arrange their social lives as they see fit; they usually have large and orderly houses suitable for entertaining. Caregivers commented in the interviews on the social lives of their employers; one Latina woman, for example, said that her employers were "people of extreme importance" in the business world and necessarily had a lot of parties. Caregivers, in contrast, have minimal ability to organize their social lives. They do meet other caregivers in parks, but they cannot count on doing so. Occasionally these relationships deepen into real friendships, but caregivers often do not know each other's last names, even when they have met frequently, and rarely sustain friendships when their work schedules no longer bring them together.

The parents' model of sociability has been extended downward. Even very young children now have arranged social lives. The play date has replaced neighborhood gatherings. Parents are anxious for their children to play with friends, both to develop their social skills and to certify their popularity. Once children leave infancy, they acquire their own miniature social circle, generally made up of children from families much like their own. This can cause problems for caregivers. They have little or no standing in their employers' social milieu, and they can feel this acutely when dealing with other families. Parents usually initiate contact with other families, but caregivers supervise the actual visits. Many caregivers report resentment at how other parents treat them and at how visiting children feel free to order them around.

Caregivers sometimes refuse to deal with certain families if they feel they have been ill-treated. This can be frustrating for their employers; one Los Angeles doctor said regretfully that her two-year-old son could no longer play with his best friend during the week, because her African-American caregiver had had a dispute with the friend's mother and nanny. "She said that the mother was being too controlling of her. . . . She felt that this woman was dictating to her what she should do and that she wasn't employed by this woman and she had no right to tell her what to do." The nanny felt the other family's caregiver also acted in a high-handed manner. The other child had come over every Monday for the preceding year and a half, but the nanny refused to allow any more visits while she was on duty. The mother said she felt sad about the situation, but then added hopefully that the caregiver was nearing sixty and might soon retire. One Mexican caregiver told a visiting child that she would not take orders from her; the child complained to her mother, who called the caregiver's employer. The employer said, "Please, Maria, be more amiable with their friends." Maria refused, however, to agree to accept orders from the friends; she said that if they wanted anything, they could relay their requests through her charges.

Sympathetic employers sometimes back their caregivers in disputes with other parents and children. A Los Angeles professor stood behind her Guatemalan caregiver in a conflict with a neighbor, who had felt free to treat the caregiver as a servant. The professor said "she was right. And I told the neighbors she was right." Not all parents will do this, however, and if caregivers are perceived as too contentious, parents can consider firing them on this issue. They do not want caregivers' sensitivities to impede their children's social lives.

## PRESCHOOL AND OTHER
## ORGANIZED ACTIVITIES

Increasingly, parents enroll even young children in structured activities. By the time the children of the parents we interviewed were three, nearly all attended preschools, mainly on a part-time basis. Even couples who employed full-time caregivers wanted their children to have the stimulation and organized activities provided by trained teachers.

When parents enrolled their children in preschools, they initiated a major shift in socialization strategy. As their children began structured forms of learning and care, their caregivers lost influence, a process that would accelerate when the children began more formal schooling.

The parents we interviewed also reported their children participated in music lessons, dance, gymnastics, karate, special math classes, all kinds of sports activities, and art classes. Slightly older children took computer classes. Taught by specialized teachers, these classes have great legitimacy in middle-class circles. Even parents who worry that their children no longer have time for themselves said that they could not be the only holdouts: their children had no friends to play with in the neighborhood, because those children were all off at classes. They also thought that if their children did not participate in these activities, they might be left behind socially and developmentally. These classes and activities provide a form of socialization on a contract basis. Even children's academic performance can now fall within the province of experts for hire. When their children had trouble learning to read, or had difficulty with math, the parents we interviewed often hired tutors. Few contemplated tackling these problems unassisted. As children get older, unskilled caregivers play ever smaller roles, while specialists play ever larger ones.

The wealthiest parents in the study did not simply enroll their children in classes; they brought specialists to their houses. Those with pools hired private swimming instructors; an employer with a tennis court gave room and board to a tennis "hitter" so that he would be available for her children. One Los Angeles mother stretched her budget to engage a first-grade teacher from her children's public school to come to the house twice a week and give art lessons to her daughters. On Fridays after school the teacher led a group of six girls, organized by the mother, on tours of the city's art museums. The mother did not go, reasoning that at $30 an hour, it was better for her children to get the teacher's attention. Instead of sending their children to Hebrew classes a New Jersey couple had a rabbi come by twice a week.

## THE VALUES CHILDREN LEARN

Some wealthy parents take an extra step and hire multiple caregivers. With several employees, they can assemble various types of expertise within their homes. Although most employers we interviewed found that paying for, and coping with, one employee exhausted their resources, eight of the families interviewed employed multiple caregivers. Two of these hired only class subordinates; they used more than one because they had intensive labor demands (one employer, for example, required her baby to be carried around all day and also had two older children to look after; she hired two Salvadoran caregivers). The others, though, mixed class peers and class subordinates, creating a labor hierarchy like that of elites in previous generations. The highest-status workers do the most direct work with children. One Los Angeles lawyer hired many employees for help with her one son: at one time, before he started school, she had an English nanny, a Guatemalan immigrant full time, a UCLA student two mornings a week, and a regular Saturday-evening babysitter.

Children with teams of servants at their disposal sometimes develop a unique view of the world: They see all relationships as potential employment relationships. The eight-year-old son of the Los Angeles lawyer told his mother he liked some of his camp counselors and wanted her to hire them. "Right now he's in love with this one young woman and he wants her to work for us, too. I don't know how we'll use her; I have all these people already." As children get older, they recognize that caregivers are paid employees, yet many children have also experienced semi-maternal affection from them. This can create a complicated sense of how money can be used to buy emotional gratification. While these feelings may lie deeply submerged within relationships, caregivers sometimes interpret children's comments as indicating that they see their parents as having purchased caregivers for their enjoyment, just as other possessions are supplied for them.

Many employers who have egalitarian ideologies work hard to keep their children from treating caregivers disrespectfully, usually with some success. Some worry, though, that their own status as personal "dictators" cannot help influencing their children. And, whatever the children's level of respect, parents cannot keep them from becoming more distant from caregivers. Children gradually come to understand the caregivers' subordinate and temporary position, a process closely charted by the caregivers themselves; they notice small signs of children's changing regard for them. One Mexican caregiver said that the boy she looked after would include her in the pictures of his family that he drew in kindergarten. When he went to first grade, he stopped doing this. "The closeness he felt for me has grown cold. He sees me as an employee." This led her to withdraw in turn. "When he was very little, and I felt he cared for me, I felt much closer to him. Now I just see him as someone else with whom I have to work."

Caregivers whose employers do not enforce respect from children can have much worse situations. As children get older, they can come to see caregivers as their personal servants.[13] When caregivers ask them to pick up after themselves, some children tell them, "That's your job." Gradually caregivers can come to feel themselves under the control of the children who are nominally in their charge. Even caregivers who have been close to the children can come to dislike them when they assert their superiority. Adela, the Salvadoran caregiver whose employer complained she could not teach the children about art (chapter 2), had once loved the two girls in the family. But at five or six, they began telling her "You have to do this because this is why you get paid." Not only caregivers reported such treatment; some parents frankly admitted that their older children had hit or insulted caregivers. Even when treated abusively, subordinate caregivers do not feel they can strike back. One Latina woman overheard school-age boys arguing about who had the stupidest maid. She could do nothing but remain silent. This is an age-old problem for domestic workers. African-American women in the South addressed it with such sayings as "I never met a white child over twelve that I liked."[14]

In the eyes of some caregivers, the children in their charge are learning values, but not necessarily the ones officially espoused by the parents. These caregivers think the children are learning which work is done by which people. They observe how the children come to see them as employees and to recognize that they as children have more power than their adult caregivers. Few things are more painful for caregivers than to see children they once loved take a domineering tone toward them, not with the unthinking egoism of the young but with the knowing superiority of the privileged.

Children can learn an indelible lesson—just how indelible can be seen by comparing parents who grew up in families with domestic workers and those who did not. Even as adults, they respond differently to domestic employees. A few reacted against how they had seen their own parents treat workers. More commonly, those raised in a household that had domestic employees assume their right to service. They do not have to fight internal battles between inbred egalitarian and hierarchical notions; their consciousness was shaped in the hierarchical direction long before. They are re-creating the same feelings and expectations in their own children.[15]

Caregivers also know that no matter how well they perform their duties, their jobs have no future. One Salvadoran commented, "The instability of the job—one always feels it. From the moment I arrive at a home, I know that one day they will tell me to leave, thank you very much." Others are more bitter. They see the jobs as demanding love and commitment from them, but leaving parents free to dispose of them when they are no longer useful. "You get attached to these children, but at the end of the day you get thrown out of the house. You end up leaving in tears . . . but they [the employers] will send you to hell whenever they feel like it. You'll be able to do nothing but hang your head as you walk out."

## CONCLUSIONS

Most dual-career couples believe they have cultural resources of value to their children. They have partially lost one time-tested method of transmitting these resources, the full investment of mothers' time in children's care. Wanting individual attention for their children, and the convenience of a household worker for themselves, parents have tried to incorporate caregivers into socialization strategies. This leads them to many subsidiary efforts to select, control, and instruct those workers in ways that enable them to serve their purposes. All of these efforts are complicated by frequent, and deep, value differences between many of the women available to do caregiving work and the parents who hire them.

Parents can instruct caregivers in many aspects of care, and can demand that their own values be respected. Caregivers usually accept that parents have the right to set the basic child-rearing terms. Despite this, parents cannot be sure that the rules they have laid out will be followed; sometimes, it is clear, caregivers do not follow them. As they are essentially unsupervised workers, this is an issue that no system of control can easily address.

More important, there are areas of care that do not lend themselves to rules, but that involve subtle actions or judgments. Caregivers' ability to give focused attention to children can help them cross class boundaries when children are young, but it becomes an insufficient resource as children get older and cultural issues acquire more weight. The "quality" of care comes to be defined in more class-specific terms.

Caregivers are only a temporary element in most parents' socialization strategies, which increasingly involve contract-based care by specialists. As people whose emotions have been engaged, though, and whose livelihood had depended on particular families, their departures are not casual events. They have their own thoughts and insights into the meaning of their work. While parents seldom mention this, caregivers believe that the deepest lesson many children learn concerns their own entitlement.[16]

The road to high-level, well-rewarded careers passes through the educational system, and this is the road the children are being prepared to travel. Their caregivers can help them in their early years, by providing nurturance and love, but then the children transfer to the institutions and supports provided by middle-class culture. Along the way, however, they will have learned about privilege, and they will have exercised some.

# The Limits of Private Solutions to Public Problems

Hiring a caregiver has obvious appeal for busy parents trying to reconcile the demands of family and career. When problems arise in caregiving arrangements, they often seem individual, and of course, they *are* partly rooted in individual circumstances and personalities. Yet there are deeper reasons why these arrangements can founder, or at least not deliver on their promise for parents, children, or caregivers.

Parents who hire caregivers are usually confident they have chosen the highest-quality mode of paid child care. This faith ignores the intrinsic difficulties these arrangements create. Despite the prestige of private child care, parents have trouble controlling its quality or even knowing how good it is. For caregivers, the situation can be equally painful. They can have the worst of two worlds. They mimic mothers, but without their authority and freedom, and they are paid employees, but without the status this suggests.

Most caregiving arrangements fall somewhere in a middle

range of satisfaction to both sides. There are genuinely trusting, positive relationships between parents and caregivers, where individual attachment overcomes differences in background and position. There are many others, though, that end in firings or abrupt departures. In the continual reshuffling of employees and employers, people struggle for compatible matches, but often fail to find them. Even in positive matches, caregivers can sound a note of caution. The caregiver in one of the best employment relationships encountered in the study said of her employer: "She has always treated me well. So far." With no security, caregivers can take nothing for granted.

These caregiving arrangements basically turn the clock back to earlier forms of dependency and hierarchy. They also lead parents to accommodate to negative social conditions, rather than to challenge them. Many women have entered male-dominated workplaces where the needs of parents have received short shrift. Many operate within families where gender equality is honored more in principle than in practice. When parents hire caregivers, they finesse, rather than address, these issues. By delegating child care, they are able to put in the long hours required by rigid workplaces. Mothers have less reason to press fathers for equal participation if someone else is doing the work. By buying other people's labor, dual-career parents can individually exempt themselves from larger social problems. Their private solutions, though, bring their own problems, and they limit pressure for broader changes.

## QUALITY OF CARE

When parents hire caregivers, they embed child care in unequal relationships. They wield power over the women who provide the care. This affects who will do the work, how they feel about doing it, and the kind of care they offer. Proponents of in-home care see it as similar to a mother's care, but no middle-class mother would work under the conditions of private caregivers. Paid care differs decisively from family care, despite taking place in the children's home under the parents' direction.

Quality care depends on motivated workers who have initiative, yet many caregivers face working conditions that undermine commitment. Unlike parents, caregivers do not control their own working conditions. Mothers who acknowledge that being with young children all day would drive them crazy can expect caregivers to endure it without protest or perhaps even inner resistance. On some level, many dual-career couples see caregivers as having simpler needs than they themselves do and thus as being better at tolerating monotony.

An agency owner put it simply: People can't give unless they get. Not all caregivers get much in the way of money, companionship, or diversion. Because caregivers work, and often live, on other people's turf, normal social outlets are closed to them. Their jobs do not provide peer companionship, of the kind middle-class people expect from their own workplaces. There is no office gossip to be shared, no politicking to be done. Some are lucky; they find other nannies in the neighborhood and socialize in parks and up and down the block. Those who work for flexible or trusting parents create variety by planning their own days. But most parents do not want caregivers to enjoy this degree of freedom. They worry that their children will be dragged around on errands, that they could be brought into unsafe situations, or that caregivers will pursue their own goals rather than concentrating on the children's needs. These are legitimate concerns. Nonetheless, they can result in caregivers' working in aching isolation and boredom. Parents with normal gumption and social drive would not tolerate days so bleak. They would invite friends over, grab the kids and go for excursions, or sign up for playgroups or "Mommy and Me" classes. Social commentators consider stay-at-home mothers' isolation the Achilles heel of suburban living, but caregivers suffer much more from this than do mothers themselves.[1]

Parents say, and to some extent caregivers accept, that because caregivers are paid and mothers are not, it is reasonable for working conditions to differ. One mother said about her caregiver: "When she's on duty and working, she's working, you know. She's not just trying to get through a day, like a parent would." Her caregiver, though, like most others, worked from early in the day, when she made the children breakfast, until the evening, when she finished the dinner dishes. In a sense, parents want it both ways. They want caregivers to approach their jobs with the same serious purpose people bring to most paid employment. They should not need diversion. Yet parents also expect caregivers to accept much longer hours than are normal in paid work.

Caregivers can spend so much time alone with young children that they say they almost lose the capacity to speak normally with adults. The most socially deprived literally have no one to talk to outside their employers' family. One young woman from Grenada who has worked for a year for a suburban New Jersey family, looking after their two school-age boys, cleans for a few hours after the boys depart for school and the parents for work, then has to fill the time until the boys get home. After dinner, she spends her evenings in her windowless basement room. She does not know of any other nannies nearby and she has yet to see another black person in the neighborhood. With no access to a car (and no chance of getting a driver's license, as she is in the country illegally), she can roam only as far as she can walk. A naturally buoyant person, she does not know how much longer she can sustain herself.

These harsh working conditions can lead to depression, and they certainly provide little relief for those who are already depressed. Caregivers differ greatly in their personalities and degrees of cheer, but a substantial minority of those interviewed seemed sad. Women who run households, and au pairs with active social lives, are generally the most cheerful; some thrive and describe their experiences as wonderful. Male au pairs can do splendidly, often generating large social networks. Young immigrant women in low-level jobs, in contrast, seemed particularly lonely and needy, especially those living in employers' houses. Deprived of companionship, or even of the small freedoms accorded most adults, such as the right to take food out of the refrigerator when they feel like it, they can become somber and withdrawn.

Depression can be the enemy of good child care, as it reduces people's ability to respond to children with humor or interest.[2] In the most serious cases, this can have observable effects on children. One Los Angeles mother hired an older Mexican caregiver whose personal life was grim: she had left Mexico partly to escape an alcoholic and abusive husband. The mother said she later found out the caregiver was "super depressed." The caregiver's husband

> did terrible things to her self-esteem. She didn't talk much and I found out later that it was not a good idea to have my child who was learning to speak with someone who didn't want to talk. She did everything she was supposed to do in terms of being there and he was safe, but I was really concerned because my child was two and a half, three, and not talking.

The parents took their son to a university clinic to have him evaluated. The psychologists told them the child needed more stimulation and advised the parents to get him in the company of other children and of normally cheerful adults. The mother felt sympathy for the caregiver, but was even more saddened that her son's development appeared to have been set back.

One expert says the "well-developing" child between nine months and two years usually speaks to the adults around him or her ten times an hour.[3] The child does best when adults respond in complete sentences, in words at or just above the child's comprehension level. This is quite a lot of talk, particularly since much of it is of little intrinsic interest to adults. A day spent actively talking with a two-year-old is much more tiring than one simply spent in that child's company. Hired caregivers who get little emotional replenishment themselves, who may be with young children for ten or twelve hours a day, can have a particularly hard time summoning the energy to actively engage with children.

Parents have almost no power to control this aspect of care. No one can be forced to talk to another person, and certainly not when the "supervisors," the parents, are not even there most of the day. Truly committed, engaged, thoughtful care can come only from employees who want to do a good job (and who share the parents' definition of good care). To the extent that caregivers work in more draining and boring circumstances than the parents themselves, parents increase the likelihood of getting routinized and limited care, as opposed to more playful, active, stimulating companionship for their children.

Perhaps because of class-related assumptions about what people need in life, even well-meaning parents can expect more of class-subordinate caregivers than they expect of themselves. The large supply of immigrant women willing to do these jobs means parents can largely determine caregivers' working conditions. They can, in fact, find women who will work twelve hours a day for a low wage and who will endure social isolation. Whether this leads to good care is another matter.

## WHEN BEING A BOSS TAKES OVER

When parents hire caregivers, they change their household dynamics. They have become employers. They do not want to be taken advantage of; they want their caregivers to work productively, without being too much trouble to themselves. These relatively simple goals can be hard to meet. Parents can find themselves engaged in disconcerting power struggles. Over time, those struggles can acquire a life of their own and edge out larger goals.

Caregivers are brought onto employers' turf, so parents face basic issues about how much of the caregivers' behavior to try to control. With live-in workers, some parents go far down this road, seeing caregivers as needing permission to use supplies or appliances in the home. One live-in Mexican caregiver in Los Angeles said she had bought herself vegetables, as she wanted to go on a diet. When her employer began eating the vegetables, the caregiver said, "But that's my food." The employer replied, "But it's my refrigerator." This is the "boss" perspective in crude form. Even employees with more standing can be uneasy about what they can and can't do in their employers' houses. They can become anxious about the telephone, and in fact, some employers do forbid caregivers to receive calls, or they set remarkably specific controls on phone use: one employer of an Irish nanny told her she could receive calls for a specified fifteen-minute period each day.

Most parents are not this restrictive, but caregivers are aware that they have the power to be. They can tell live-in caregivers what time to get home at night; who can visit and when; and, to a considerable degree, when and what they can eat. Denied adult freedoms, caregivers in restrictive households occupy an intermediate status, not children but not full adults either. They have a lot of responsibility, but in their daily lives they can be denied normal symbols of respect and trust. They not only do not control their working conditions, many do not control their living conditions. An agency observer summed up their predicament, saying "I've never had a boss I wanted to live with."

Some caregivers can see the struggles their employers go through trying to decide how to treat them. A woman from Guyana felt her employer was internally conflicted: "Sometimes she gets a little confused. 'Should I get close to my nanny? Should I not get close? Should I be autocratic? Should I be a show-off in the presence of my friends? Should I sit on the beach and read my law book in my deck chair and have my nanny run behind my kid?'"

The caregiver added that the mother "had a self-esteem problem" that led her to assert her superiority. It hurt, the nanny said, but she tried not to let it bother her.

The more employers try to control, the more room for conflict. Even employers who do not believe they should run their caregivers' lives can find themselves in disputes over matters peripheral to child care. These disputes take an emotional toll; caregivers, in particular, can become alienated and angry over them, which can affect their attitude toward the children in their charge.

Parents may feel deeply that their children's welfare is their top priority, but when they become angry or frustrated by their caregivers, other issues can come first. It is not uncommon for parents to refuse to allow departing caregivers a chance to say good-bye to children they may have looked after for months, or even years. Parents can order them out, without regard for their children's feelings.

Children learn from what they see around them as well as from what they are taught. They see their parents acting as bosses, and they can become small bosses in turn. Highly privileged members of society can develop a "deep-seated feeling of superiority [that] often has its origins in youngsters being catered to by servants and local merchants."[4] Many caregivers described their pain as children began to order them around. A caregiver commented on this: "It makes you feel horrible. It makes you feel bad as a person and if you can't deal with it and get over that very quickly, then you can become very depressed on the job. And what parents don't know is, if you're not happy on the job, you can't take care of those children well." Children see who does which work, and which work is most valued. The household comes to mirror larger social inequalities.

## DISTANCING OF PARENTS AND CHILDREN

Caregivers affect family dynamics in ways other forms of child care do not. Not only do children see their parents asserting authority over caregivers, but the caregivers' presence can affect how parents themselves act toward their children.[5] Basically, when live-in caregivers are present, parents can slide toward doing less and less with their children. This tendency isn't seen in parents who send their children to day care centers. The parents have to pick them up by specific times. They have to eat dinner with them, because there is no alternative. This is not true for parents who hire live-in caregivers. They discover many tasks involve a choice. They can choose to have dinner with their children, or not. They can choose to spend the evening with them, or not.

Some parents who employ live-in caregivers see their children only minimally. They have their babies sleep in the caregiver's room; they come home from work only an hour or so before their children go to bed. There are people who never eat a meal with their children during the week. During the summer some parents send even very young children to country houses with caregivers, appearing only intermittently themselves.

Even highly motivated parents can discover that caregivers offer them a luxurious level of personal freedom. In limited doses, this is clearly beneficial. One professor, who hired a caregiver only because her husband made it a condition for their having children, said that she adjusted to the arrangement. "The nightmare of early childhood was no nightmare for me." She could play tennis whenever she chose and could come and go from her home without a thought. Parents commonly find themselves unloading more child-rearing duties than they first expect. A mother of two daughters, ages three and one, said of her caregiver: "We let her feed them dinner, although we really felt, originally very strongly, that families should have dinner together and children should be a part of dinner. It's better in theory than in fact. It was too much, too hectic. So now she feeds them." When already paid-for labor is available, it takes a strong-minded parent to keep shouldering the work.

Caregivers are not a neutral or inert presence; they affect many different aspects of family relationships. By and large, they do not enhance the closeness of parents and children. Not only do parents leave them tasks they used to do with and for their children, but the caregivers can engage in some level of emotional competition with mothers. It is a competition which, in the long run, they are bound to lose, but they can put up a fight in the short run.

The most sophisticated and thoughtful caregivers do not try to outshine their employers. They say that if they see a child take his first steps, for example, they remain silent. They let the parents see it for themselves. When children call them "Mommy," they explain they are not their mothers. But not all caregivers are this noble. Some, with few sources of ego gratification, actively encourage children to declare their preference for them. At the least, they take pride in children's declarations of love; many said in interviews that the children loved them at least as much as they loved their parents. This, again, is not an issue that arises with other forms of child care, or only very marginally.

## REINFORCING THE STATUS QUO

As middle-class mothers have gone to work, many have fought gender inequality. They would like to restructure both their households and their workplaces. Most have run up against a wall on both fronts.[6] Men have proved resistant to taking on household tasks and child care. Many husbands point to their careers as reason for not doing more. Men's careers are still often accorded priority in two-career families. This emerged in interview after interview. In describing their families' daily schedules, the women often said they left for work later than their husbands and returned earlier. Some essentially put their careers on hold when their children were infants.

By hiring caregivers, these women avoided the tensions and conflicts that can arise when women really push men toward more equal participation. They basically turned gender inequalities into class inequalities. Similarly, caregivers reduced the tension between work and family demands. Parents in professional careers can be called upon for night and weekend work; they can be expected to travel. Jobs are structured for men with at-home wives looking after the children. Those women who did not reduce the demands of their own careers relied on caregivers to help them survive—sometimes just barely—the multiple claims on them.

Professionally employed women often said they loved their work, but felt angry and conflicted about how hard it was to combine their jobs with their family lives. A Los Angeles lawyer described a bad few years after her first child was born: "There was a period of time where I felt awful. I felt like people considered me useless. When I was home I felt guilty, when I was at the office I felt guilty. I really had a hard time of it." This woman stayed home for three months with her child, but paid a high price emotionally and professionally. Only after she made a splash with an intellectual-property case three years after her daughter's birth did she feel welcomed back into her firm.

Demand for professional commitment can be so great that some women are afraid even to ask for extra time off when their children are born. An investment banker who had twins took a three-month leave; she wanted to stay with them longer, but thought the career penalty would be too great: "I could have asked for more time, but women in my business who have done that, their careers have almost ended." This woman was not being paranoid; researchers have found that women pay a high price when they step out of their careers and then try to return.[7] The

United States lacks family-friendly policies found in Western European countries, such as paid parental leaves.[8] A lawyer was stunned by her male partners' negative attitudes when she wanted to be with her new baby. They told her they had not taken time off. "They've said that to me. 'No, we all had children, what's the problem?' Their wives don't work. They go home when they feel like it. They see the kid once a week."

Some regret their career decisions, because they entail such sacrifice of family life. A surgeon said she now thinks her career choice was stupid. "You can't imagine years of working seven days a week." She now has a successful practice, but she says, "I think of quitting every day." She envies women who work normal hours. Her husband, also a surgeon, works even longer hours than she does. The saving grace for them is their capable, cheerful Jamaican housekeeper, who runs their household. Even so, this mother says she wishes she had someone a step above the housekeeper, who could function as a quasi-wife.

Caregivers take on such a range of tasks that husbands and wives do not have to fully confront the gender inequalities remaining. Similarly, when caregivers adapt to parents' work schedules, the parents' employers do not have to face challenges to their time-honored ways of structuring their employees' days and careers. Caregivers add enough social fluidity to households to limit pressure for gender equality and for work restructuring. They help solve individual problems, while leaving social problems intact.

## A BROADER AGENDA

Today there is little organized pressure for high-quality, government-monitored group day care. Although this was one of the earliest demands of the second wave of American feminism, it has slipped into the background. Women do not stand united on this issue, in part because those with the most power and social influence often choose another form of care. Group care becomes irrelevant to them.[9]

Some women who hired caregivers said they would have used day care had good centers been available to them, but most spoke negatively of group care. They saw it as cold and impersonal. They thought that in hiring caregivers, they were buying their children a far higher quality of care. Negative feelings about day care emerged strongly in an interview with a Los Angeles mother. When she was asked about her son's preschool, the boy himself piped up that he had not liked it. It was, he said, like day care. His mother cried out, "Oh, no, no, no, no." Even if imperfect, the preschool was not that low.

In the United States, day care centers still struggle to overcome the stigma of having originated for poor children.[10] While parents gain prestige when they hire caregivers, in privileged circles they can be viewed as bad parents if their children go to day care centers, although this is less true for academics than for those in the corporate world.

If, however, good care comes most easily from people whose own needs are met—needs for job security, for benefits, for companionship, for growth—day care centers offer clear advantages as employers over parents. Day care teachers are poorly paid,[11] but they stand above caregivers in salary, security, and training. They also do not face conflicts between meeting the needs of parents and of children. They are not personal servants, but independently employed professionals. In the evenings, they do not retire to single rooms to sit in front of TV sets, as too many live-in domestic workers must do; instead, they can organize their time and social lives as they see fit.

Many outstanding women work as caregivers in private homes. They display remarkable commitment and energy in jobs with limited rewards. The question is whether child care should be recognized as socially valuable work, where people get treated well for doing it, earning respect and decent incomes. The chances of securing this in the private market are limited. For many workers, the organization of the private market does not improve their skills and commitment; if anything, it reduces them. Working in bad conditions, under the personal control of employers, and often left isolated and unsupervised, caregivers struggle on as best they can, but that best may not translate into quality care. A move toward a system of good child care requires recognition that private child care solutions cannot solve social problems.

# *Notes*

1. The data come from the weighted primary age sample of the 1991 National Household Education Survey (Washington, D.C.: National Center for Education Statistics). The figure in the text refers to the question on whether the parents had ever used care by a nonrelative in the child's own home. If they answered "yes" or "both" (care by nonrelative in the child's own home and another person's home), they were coded as having used in-home care.

   Child care experts note that in-home care accounts for only a small part of total care: see, for example, Cheryl D. Hayes, John L. Palmer, and Martha J. Zaslow, eds., *Who Cares for America's Children? Child Care Policy for the 1990s* (Washington, D.C.: National Academy Press, 1990), p. 150. This is true; about 6 percent of parents in the National Household Education Survey say they have ever used this kind of care. Nannies or babysitters are disproportionately hired by middle-class and wealthy families, though, and by parents with high levels of education. Almost a third of parents with advanced degrees have hired in-home caregivers. These socially influential parents have considerable capacity to shape social policy debates on child care. Further, as these are the parents with the greatest freedom to choose the kind of care they want, their heavy use of in-home care suggests other parents would also hire nannies if they thought they could afford it.

2. Alison Clarke-Stewart, *Daycare*, rev. ed. (Cambridge, Mass.: Harvard University Press, 1993), p. 43.

3. Most of the interviews (including all those with caregivers) were conducted between 1989 and 1994; a small number of employer interviews were conducted in 1987 and 1988.

4. Those interviewed included twenty-four doctors (plus six others in medical fields), thirty-one lawyers, and fourteen professors or academic researchers. Twenty-one parents worked as managers or owners of business enterprises. Others worked in art, music, or design (eight), or were contractors (five), computer consultants (five), or therapists of various sorts (four). Others worked for nonprofit organizations (four), or worked in the film or television industries (six). In ones or twos there were architects, writers, journalists, ministers, CPAs, and people in such miscellaneous occupations as airline representative.

5. Ninety-three percent of the parents interviewed graduated from college (and all except one had at least some college); 62 percent had graduate or profes-

sional degrees. In sixty of the seventy-nine families, the mothers worked outside the home. Forty-one of these women worked full-time and nineteen worked part-time. Nineteen women did not work outside the home at the time of the interview; many of these women had decided to stay home after the births of second or third children.

6. To my knowledge, this is the first time information has been systematically gathered from employers and employees in the same relationship. For a unique and sensitive look at servants' lives written by a son of their employers, who went back and interviewed the servants when he was an adult, see Ronald Fraser, *In Search of a Past: The Manor House, Annersfield, 1933–1945* (London: Verso, 1984).

7. The data are from the 1990 Public Use Microdata Samples for New York and Los Angeles. The data relate to workers in three categories of private-household occupations: private-household cleaners and servants; housekeepers and butlers; and child care workers. Male workers were excluded; they formed only a tiny percentage, and we did not want to include butlers. The great majority of immigrant caregivers also do housework, so it is not clear that they would describe themselves simply as "child care workers" as opposed to "household cleaners and servants," which is why we included all three occupational categories. Also, the interviews show that workers quite commonly switch back and forth between house cleaning and child care, so they are not entirely distinct occupations.

8. The large number of Central Americans in Los Angeles is a relatively recent phenomenon. On migration from Central America in the wake of wars and violence, see Guy Gugliotta, "The Central American Exodus: Grist for the Migrant Mill," in *The Caribbean Exodus,* ed. Barry B. Levine (New York: Praeger, 1987), pp. 171–82.

9. Englewood also has a working-class population, but all the employers interviewed came from the town's geographically distinct middle-class area.

10. Dolores Trevizo wrote her master's thesis ("Latina 'Baby Watchers' and the Commodification of Care," Department of Sociology, UCLA, 1990) on caregivers, based on an initial sample of interviews.

*Chapter 1. The Parents' Dilemma*

1. Rosanna Hertz, *More Equal Than Others: Women and Men in Dual-Career Marriages* (Berkeley: University of California Press, 1986), pp. 147–95, discusses dual-career couples and their preference for hiring nannies.

2. Alison Clarke-Stewart, *Daycare,* rev. ed. (Cambridge, Mass.: Harvard University Press, 1993), p. 28.

3. There is a large literature attacking group child care. See, for example, Deborah Fallows, *A Mother's Work* (Boston: Houghton Mifflin, 1985), and Wendy Dreskin and William Dreskin, *The Day Care Decision: What's Best for Your Child* (New York: M. Evans, 1983). On the wave of sexual-abuse allegations, see Joel Best, *Threatened Children: Rhetoric and Concern about Child Victims* (Chicago: University of Chicago Press, 1990), p. 73.

4. Joanne Lipman, "The Nanny Trap," *Wall Street Journal,* April 14, 1993, p. 1.

5. David E. Rosenbaum, "Usually, the Illegality in Domestic Work Is Benefits Denied," *New York Times,* January 31, 1993, section 4, p. 5.

6. *Newsweek,* October 11, 1993, p. 6. In October 1994, Congress revised the rules regarding tax payments for nannies and other household employees. The new law reduced the paperwork, as well as raising the earnings threshold for Social Security taxes. "The Nanny Tax, Improved," *New York Times,* October 7, 1994, p. A30.

7. Judge Kimba Wood had not broken any laws, but the Clinton administration still jettisoned her, claiming that she had not been forthright with staffers about her nanny situation.

8. Jennifer Senior, "In Washington, Au Pairs Are Bipartisan Choice for Child Care," *New York Times,* April 21, 1994, p. C9. On a political candidate being attacked for employing an undocumented nanny, see B. Drummond Ayres, Jr., "California GOP Candidate Admits Hiring Illegal Alien," *New York Times,* October 28, 1994, pp. A1, A27.

9. There is a large literature on social-class differences in child-rearing values: see, for example, Melvin L. Kohn, *Class and Conformity: A Study in Values,* 2nd ed. (Chicago: University of Chicago Press, 1977); Melvin Kohn, Atsushi Naoi, Carrie Schoenbach, Carmi Schooler, and Kazimierz Slomczynski, "Position in the Class Structure and Psychological Functioning in the United States, Japan, and Poland," *American Journal of Sociology* 95 (1990): 964–1008; Duane F. Alwin, "Social Stratification, Conditions of Work, and Parental Socialization Values," in *Social and Moral Values: Individual and Societal Perspectives,* ed. Nancy Eisenberg, Janusz Reykowski, and Ervin Staub (Hillsdale, N.J.: Erlbaum, 1989), pp. 327–46.

10. On race and domestic work, see Mary Romero, *Maid in the U.S.A.* (New York: Routledge, 1992); Phyllis Palmer, *Domesticity and Dirt: Housewives and Domestic Servants in the United States, 1920–1945* (Philadelphia: Temple University Press, 1989); Evelyn Nakano Glenn, "Racial Ethnic Women's Labor: The Intersection of Race, Gender, and Class Oppression," in *Gender, Family, and Economy: The Triple Overlap,* ed. Rae Lesser Blumberg (Newbury Park, Calif.: Sage, 1991), pp. 173–201; Evelyn Nakano Glenn, *Issei, Nisei, War Bride: Three Generations of Japanese American Women in Domestic Service* (Philadelphia: Temple University Press, 1986); Bonnie Thornton Dill, "Across the Boundaries of Race and Class: An Exploration of the Relationship between Work and Family Among Black Female Domestic Servants" (Ph.D. diss., New York University, 1979); Judith Rollins, *Between Women: Domestics and Their Employers* (Philadelphia: Temple University Press, 1985); Shellee Colen, "'Just a Little Respect': West Indian Domestic Workers in New York City," in *Muchachas No More: Household Workers in Latin America and the Caribbean,* ed. Elsa M. Chaney and Mary Garcia Castro (Philadelphia: Temple University Press, 1989), pp. 171–94; and Susan Tucker, *Telling Memories Among Southern Women: Domestic Workers and Their Employers in the Segregated South* (Baton Rouge: Louisiana State University Press, 1988).

11. Nancy Foner, "The Jamaicans: Race and Ethnicity Among Migrants in New York City," in *New Immigrants in New York,* ed. Nancy Foner (New York: Columbia University Press, 1987), pp. 195–217.

12. U.S. Bureau of the Census, 1990 Public Use Microdata Samples, New York.

13. Pamela Horn, *The Rise and Fall of the Victorian Servant* (New York: St. Martin's Press, 1975); Jonathan Gathorne-Hardy, *The Rise and Fall of the British*

*Nanny* (London: Hodder and Stoughton, 1972); B. W. Lorence, "Parents and Children in Eighteenth-Century Europe," *History of Childhood Quarterly: Journal of Psychohistory* 1 (1974): 1–30; Randolph Trumbach, *The Rise of the Egalitarian Family: Aristocratic Kinship and Domestic Relations in Eighteenth-Century England* (London: Academic Press, 1978).

14. M. Jeanne Peterson, "The Victorian Governess: Status Incongruence in Family and Society," in *Suffer and Be Still: Women in the Victorian Age,* ed. Martha Vicinus (Bloomington: Indiana University Press, 1973), pp. 3–19.

15. Gathorne-Hardy, *The Rise and Fall of the British Nanny,* p. 71.

16. See Cissie Fairchilds, *Domestic Enemies: Servants and Their Masters in Old Regime France* (Baltimore: Johns Hopkins University Press, 1984), on how children could come to identify with their family's servants; Gathorne-Hardy, *The Rise and Fall of the British Nanny,* pp. 216–29.

17. Julia Wrigley, "Servants and Cultural Transmission Within English Families." Paper presented at the annual meeting of the American Sociological Association, San Francisco, August 1989.

18. Joseph Priestley, *Miscellaneous Observations Relating to Education, More Especially as It Respects the Conduct of the Mind* (Millwood, N.Y.: Kraus Reprint Company, 1977 [1796]).

19. Maria Edgeworth and Richard Lovell Edgeworth, *Practical Education* (Boston: Samuel Parker, 1823), p. 13.

20. Randall Collins, *The Credential Society* (New York: Academic Press, 1979); Joel Perlmann, *Ethnic Differences: Schooling and Social Structure Among the Irish, Italians, Jews & Blacks in an American City, 1880–1935* (Cambridge: Cambridge University Press, 1988).

21. Annette Lareau, *Home Advantage: Social Class and Parental Intervention in Elementary Education* (London: Falmer Press, 1989).

22. Shirley Brice Heath, *Ways with Words: Language, Life, and Work in Communities and Classrooms* (Cambridge: Cambridge University Press, 1983).

23. Julia Wrigley, "Do Young Children Need Intellectual Stimulation? Experts' Advice to Parents, 1900–1985," *History of Education Quarterly* 29 (1989): 41–75.

24. Burton L. White, *The First Three Years of Life,* 2nd ed. (New York: Simon & Schuster, 1993).

25. David Elkind, *The Hurried Child* (Reading, Mass.: Addison-Wesley, 1981).

26. Barbara Ehrenreich, *Fear of Falling: The Inner Life of the Middle Class* (New York: Harper Perennial, 1989), p. 83.

27. Katherine S. Newman, *Falling from Grace: The Experience of Downward Mobility in the American Middle Class* (New York: Vintage, 1988).

28. Pierre Bourdieu and J. C. Passeron, *Reproduction in Education, Society, and Culture* (Beverly Hills, Calif.: Sage, 1977).

29. Barbara Heyns, *Summer Learning and the Effects of Schooling* (New York: Academic Press, 1978).

30. Yossi Shavit and Hans-Peter Blossfeld, eds., *Persistent Inequality: Changing Educational Attainment in Thirteen Countries* (Boulder, Colo.: Westview Press, 1993).

31. Robert A. LeVine, "Women's Schooling, Patterns of Fertility, and Child Survival," *Educational Researcher* 16 (1987): 21–27.

32. Arlie Hochschild with Anne Machung, *The Second Shift: Working Parents and*

*the Revolution at Home* (New York: Viking, 1989); Scott J. South and Glenna Spitze, "Housework in Marital and Nonmarital Households," *American Sociological Review* 59 (1994): 327–47; Harriet B. Presser, "Employment Schedules Among Dual-Earner Spouses and the Division of Household Labor by Gender," ibid., 348–64.

33. See Barbara J. Berg, *The Crisis of the Working Mother: Resolving the Conflict Between Family and Work* (New York: Summit Books, 1986), pp. 70–75, on mothers' jealousy of caregivers.

*Chapter 2. Choosing Difference*

1. Most people with a choice leave the occupation. This fact emerged in a study of three types of workers in Los Angeles in the early 1980s: undocumented Mexican immigrants; legal Mexican immigrants; and native-born workers of Mexican parentage. Only undocumented immigrant women did domestic service in any numbers. Even those workers just one step above them—the legal Mexican immigrants—were rarely in the occupation. David M. Heer, *Undocumented Mexicans in the United States,* American Sociological Association Rose Monograph Series (Cambridge: Cambridge University Press, 1990), p. 147. Not all workers are able to leave, though, confined partly by undocumented status or lack of English skills. The jobs open to such workers are limited, so they improve their position more by rising within occupations than by switching from one type of work to another. Kevin F. McCarthy and R. Burciaga Valdez, *Current and Future Effects of Mexican Immigration in California* (Santa Monica, Calif.: Rand, May 1986), p. 34.

2. Shellee Colen, "'Just a Little Respect': West Indian Domestic Workers in New York City," in *Muchachas No More: Household Workers in Latin America and the Caribbean,* ed. Elsa M. Chaney and Mary Garcia Castro (Philadelphia: Temple University Press, 1989), pp. 172–73.

3. It often takes many years before the women are in a position to retrieve their children. They have to save enough money to switch to live-out status, which requires renting an apartment. They must then pay to return to their home countries; coming back to the United States, those who enter the country illegally must pay coyotes (guides) to help them and their children across the border. This can run into many hundreds of dollars. The women reported paying coyotes very different amounts (ranging from $300 for a Mexican to $3,000 for a Salvadoran). For comparison, see the discussion of coyotes and their costs in Heer, *Undocumented Mexicans in the United States,* pp. 20–21.

4. Arlie Hochschild with Anne Machung, *The Second Shift: Working Parents and the Revolution at Home* (New York: Viking, 1989).

5. Mary Romero, *Maid in the U.S.A.* (New York: Routledge, 1992), p. 117, discusses the negative effects of domestic workers' not having private space: "Although domestics are expected to create and to respect the private space of employers and their families, they themselves are denied privacy. . . . The combination of not having a bedroom and not having access to the rest of the house for resting or leisure activity continually affirms the worker's inferior status in the employer's home."

6. A New York mother described going to an employment agency where women were lined up waiting to be selected by prospective employers. The job candidates had suitcases with them so they could immediately go to the employers' houses.

7. See Romero, *Maid in the U.S.A.,* for an excellent discussion of Chicana house-cleaners' struggles to control the work process. She concludes, "Faced with lim-ited job opportunities, Chicanas turn to domestic service and restructure the occupation to resemble a businesslike arrangement" (p. 160). The workers she interviewed differed from those in this study in doing cleaning rather than child care; in addition, all were American citizens, all except one spoke English, and all did day work. Most were not the sole support of their families. These differ-ences may account for their relative success in controlling their working condi-tions, as compared to the domestic workers we interviewed. Romero notes that the Chicana women in her study had different experiences from many other women of color working as domestics (p. 147).

8. Not all the women would prefer housecleaning to child care; some find cleaning too physically demanding, and others enjoy being around children.

9. Heer, *Undocumented Mexicans in the United States,* p. 124.

10. Cheryl D. Hayes, John L. Palmer, and Martha J. Zaslow, eds., *Who Cares for America's Children? Child Care Policy for the 1990s* (Washington, D.C.: National Academy Press, 1990), p. 123.

11. Evelyn Nakano Glenn describes similar anxiety among Japanese American domestic workers about accidentally breaking employers' possessions in *Issei, Nisei, War Bride: Three Generations of Japanese American Women in Domestic Service* (Philadelphia: Temple University Press, 1986), p. 173.

12. See Caroline Zinsser, *Raised in East Urban: Child Care Changes in a Work-ing-Class Community* (New York: Teachers College Press, 1991), pp. 65–66, for an account of how white working-class babysitters in a Northeastern city also focused on the physical care of the children in their charge.

13. On class-related language differences, see Shirley Brice Heath, *Ways with Words: Language, Life, and Work in Communities and Classrooms* (Cambridge: Cambridge University Press, 1983).

14. Kevin F. McCarthy and R. Burciaga Valdez, *Current and Future Effects of Mexi-can Immigration in California* (Santa Monica, Calif.: Rand, May 1986), p. 34.

15. Domestic workers whose children are with them in the United States face very difficult circumstances. They usually work such long hours that it is very hard for them to look after their own children. These women managed in different ways. Several who had babies born in the United States had the children live with them at their employers' houses, an arrangement that became strained as the children got older. Caregivers said they became dis-turbed by the contrast between the employers' lifestyle and that which their children would experience. They also did not want their children to feel infe-rior to the wealthy children around them.

Four caregivers with children kept live-in jobs but had their children live separately from them in the United States. One child stayed with a friend for a year; in two families the fathers looked after the children; and in the fourth, two teenage children stayed in an apartment by themselves during the week and were joined by their mother on weekends. Caregivers under-standably expressed pain and anxiety about these arrangements, finding it very difficult to have their children live near them and yet be inaccessible most of the week. Even young children could be on their own a great deal; a live-in Guatemalan caregiver, who felt "sad and lonely" that she could see her children only on weekends, knew her six- and eight-year-old boys were untended after school until her husband got home. The younger boy became critically ill with a burst appendix while on his own. He had called his mother to tell her he had a stomach ache, but she did not think she could leave work. After this crisis, she switched to a live-out job.

Caregivers who lived out enjoyed much better circumstances, but they still had to find child care, a tough challenge on their meager incomes. They left children with friends and neighbors, but often did not feel they could pay them adequately. A Guatemalan caregiver in Los Angeles, for example, left her one-year-old daughter with a friend while she worked. She herself earned $200 a week; she paid her friend $40 a week to look after her baby from 7:30 in the morning until 6:00 at night. Another Guatemalan left her baby with an elderly neighbor, but was distressed that the child was not allowed to move around, as the apartment was very crowded. Even worse, when she picked him up one day she had to brush cockroaches off his clothes. Not surprisingly, it creates emotional conflicts in women to spend their days attending to other people's children while they know their own are receiving marginal care. And, of course, live-out caregivers with children face a true "second shift," with child care and housecleaning awaiting them when they get home.

16. Alejandro Portes and Ruben G. Rumbaut, *Immigrant America: A Portrait* (Berkeley: University of California Press, 1990), p. 87, discuss how whole groups of immigrants can be stereotyped as suitable only for low-wage, menial labor. On the denigration of subordinated workers and their child care capacities, note the comment of Frances Anne Kemble, the British wife of a Southern slaveowner but a critic of slavery, in *Journal of a Residence on a Georgia Plantation in 1838–1839* (New York: Knopf, 1984), p. 279:

> While the men discussed about this matter, Mrs. B[ryan] favored me with the congratulations I have heard so many times on the subject of my having a white nurserymaid for my children. Of course, she went into the old subject of the utter incompetency of Negro women to discharge such an office faithfully; but, in spite of her multiple examples of their utter inefficiency, I believe the discussion ended by simply our both agreeing that ignorant Negro girls twelve years old are not as capable or trustworthy as well-trained white women of thirty.

I am indebted to Patricia J. Williams, *The Alchemy of Race and Rights: Diary of a Law Professor* (Cambridge, Mass.: Harvard University Press, 1991) p. 239, for the citation.

17. Alison Clarke-Stewart, *Daycare,* rev. ed. (Cambridge, Mass.: Harvard University Press, 1993), p. 97.

## *Chapter 3. Choosing Similarity*

1. David Popenoe, *Disturbing the Nest: Family Change and Decline in Modern Societies* (New York: Aldine de Gruyter, 1988).

2. James Coates, "Young Mormon Women Much in Demand as Nannies," *Arizona Daily Star,* March 1, 1987, section E, p. 11.

3. Evelyn Nakano Glenn, "Racial Ethnic Women's Labor: The Intersection of Race, Gender, and Class Oppression," in *Gender, Family, and Economy: The Triple Overlap,* ed. Rae Lesser Blumberg (Newbury Park, Calif.: Sage, 1991), pp. 173–201; Phyllis Palmer, *Domesticity and Dirt: Housewives and Domestic Servants in the United States, 1920–1945* (Philadelphia: Temple University Press, 1989).

4. Mary Romero, *Maid in the U.S.A.* (New York: Routledge, 1992), p. 80.

5. Judith Rollins, *Between Women: Domestics and Their Employers* (Philadelphia: Temple University Press, 1985), p. 128.

## Chapter 4. The Struggle for Control

1. M. P. Baumgartner, *The Moral Order of a Suburb* (New York: Oxford University Press, 1989).

2. Shellee Colen reports that the Caribbean domestic workers she interviewed in New York sometimes experienced false accusations of theft: "'Just a Little Respect': West Indian Domestic Workers in New York City," in *Muchachas No More: Household Workers in Latin America and the Caribbean,* ed. Elsa M. Chaney and Mary Garcia Castro (Philadelphia: Temple University Press, 1989), p. 185; Evelyn Nakano Glenn found the same among Japanese-American domestic workers: *Issei, Nisei, War Bride: Three Generations of Japanese American Women in Domestic Service* (Philadelphia: Temple University Pree, 1986), p. 160.

3. Anthony Downs, "The Controversial Aspects of the Atlanta Region's Future," *Brookings Review* (Summer 1994):27–31.

4. Cheryl D. Hayes, John L. Palmer, and Martha J. Zaslow, eds., *Who Cares for America's Children? Child Care Policy in the 1990s* (Washington, D.C.: National Academy Press, 1990), p. 57.

5. While cases of abuse are rare, there are documented instances of nannies abusing and even killing children in their care. In New York, a nanny ultimately admitted that she killed a ten-month-old boy by shaking and hitting him; see "Parents of Dead Child Say They Suspected Abuse by Nanny," *New York Times,* November 10, 1993, p. B8, and, on the same case, Joseph Berger, "The Story of a Nanny, From Care to Calamity," *New York Times,* April 18, 1993, p. 40. Another caregiver in New York shook an eight-month-old boy to death (Raymond Hernandez, "Baby Sitter Charged with Shaking Baby to Death," *New York Times,* May 5, 1993, p. B2) and a Los Angeles father videotaped a nanny repeatedly hitting his two-year-old son and then throwing him to the floor (Richard Lee Colvin, "Taping a Gut Instinct," *Los Angeles Times,* September 26, 1991, pp. B1, B8). A Swiss au pair working in Westchester County was charged with pouring paint thinner on a baby and then burning him to death, but the evidence against her was weak and she was acquitted after a widely publicized trial; see Don Davis, *The Nanny Murder Trial* (New York: St. Martin's Paperbacks, 1993). See also N. R. Kleinfeld, "An Open Door to Disaster: Darker Side of Nanny Business: Children's Lives at Risk," *New York Times,* December 9, 1991, pp.

B1, B4; Anita Manning, "Nutty Nannies: Parents' Worst Nightmare," *USA Today,* January 13, 1992, pp. 1, 2D.

6. On the privacy of the middle-class home, see David Popenoe, *Disturbing the Nest: Family Change and Decline in Modern Societies* (New York: Aldine de Gruyter, 1988), pp. 72–73.

7. Lisa Anderson, "Who Keeps An Eye on the Nannies?" *Chicago Tribune,* May 29, 1988, section 5, pp. 2, 4, describes Scarr's experience; the quotation is from Sandra Scarr, *Mother Care/Other Care* (New York: Basic Books, 1984), p. 232.

## Chapter 5. Clashes in Values

1. Authors who discuss value differences between parents and child care providers, and between day care teachers and center directors, include Sally Lubeck, *Sandbox Society: Early Education in Black and White America* (London: Falmer Press, 1985); Caroline Zinsser, *Raised in East Urban: Child Care Changes in a Working-Class Community* (New York: Teachers College Press, 1991); Carole E. Joffe, *Friendly Intruders: Childcare Professionals and Family Life* (Berkeley: University of California Press, 1977); Elly Singer, *Child-Care and the Psychology of Development* (London: Routledge, 1992); Susan D. Holloway and Bruce Fuller, "The Great Child-Care Experiment: What Are the Lessons for School Improvement?" *Educational Researcher* 21 (1992): 12–19; and Deborah Stipek, Sharon Milburn, Darlene Clements, and Denise H. Daniels, "Parents' Beliefs about Appropriate Education for Young Children," *Journal of Applied Developmental Psychology* 13 (1992): 293–310. On family day care providers, see Margaret K. Nelson, *Negotiated Care: The Experience of Family Day Care Providers* (Philadelphia: Temple University Press, 1990).

2. Alison Clarke-Stewart, *Daycare,* rev. ed. (Cambridge, Mass.: Harvard University Press, 1993), p. 98.

3. Melvin L. Kohn, *Class and Conformity: A Study in Values,* 2nd ed. (Chicago: University of Chicago Press, 1977).

4. Stipek, Milburn, Clements, and Daniels, "Parents' Beliefs about Appropriate Education for Young Children."

5. Julia Wrigley, "Do Young Children Need Intellectual Stimulation? Experts' Advice to Parents, 1900–1985," *History of Education Quarterly* 29 (1989): 41–75.

6. Ralph Gardner, Jr., "The Preschool Grovel," *New York Observer,* July 4–11, 1994, p. 13.

7. Annette Lareau, *Home Advantage: Social Class and Parental Intervention in Elementary Education* (London: Falmer Press, 1989).

8. Lois Timnick and John H. Lee, "Three Children Killed When Flames Engulf Pacific Palisades Home," *Los Angeles Times,* March 21, 1989, section 1, p. 3; Tracy Wilkinson, "Fatal Fire: Neighbors Can Only Shake Heads," *Los Angeles Times,* March 22, 1989, section 2, p. 1.

9. Child care experts warn parents that they should not conceal their children's problems. "In choosing a care situation for a difficult child, you need to inform the caregiver fully of your child's idiosyncracies. If the caregiver can-

not accept most, or all, of your child's needs, then find another caregiver."
Sandra Scarr, *Mother Care/Other Care* (New York: Basic Books, 1984), p.
191. Not all parents follow this advice, though, whether from closing their
eyes to their child's problems or from a belief that caregivers should adjust to
what they find.

10. David Popenoe, *Disturbing the Nest: Family Change and Decline in Modern
    Societies* (New York: Aldine de Gruyter, 1988), p. 73.

11. Pierre Bourdieu, *Distinction: A Social Critique of the Judgment of Taste*, R.
    Nice, trans. (Cambridge: Harvard University Press, 1984).

12. Michael Argyle, *The Psychology of Social Class* (New York: Routledge, 1994),
    pp. 68–70.

13. James H. S. Bossard, *The Sociology of Child Development* (New York: Harper
    & Brothers, 1948), p. 279, discusses how the presence of servants can lead
    children to expect a high level of personal service. Bossard argues this can
    help shape the child's sense of self by creating an early sense of superiority.

14. Susan Tucker, *Telling Memories Among Southern Women: Domestic Workers
    and Their Employers in the Segregated South* (Baton Rouge: Louisiana State
    University Press, 1988), p. 61.

15. Judith Rollins found that women were much influenced by family tradition in
    hiring domestics. See *Between Women: Domestics and Their Employers*
    (Philadelphia: Temple University Press, 1985), pp. 94–102.

16. In the more extreme case of slavery, Thomas Jefferson described how chil-
    dren learned tyranny by watching their slaveowning parents:

    > The whole commerce between master and slave is a perpetual exer-
    > cise of the most boistrous passions, the most unremitting despotism on
    > the one part, and degrading submissions on the other. Our children see
    > this, and learn to imitate it. . . . If a parent could find no motive either in
    > his philanthropy or his self-love, for restraining the intemperance of pas-
    > sion towards his slave, it should always be a sufficient one that the child
    > is present. But generally it is not sufficient. The parent storms, the child
    > looks on, catches the lineaments of wrath, puts on the same airs in the
    > circle of smaller slaves, gives a loose to his worst of passions, and thus
    > nursed, educated, and daily exercised in tyranny, cannot but be stamped
    > by it with odious peculiarities.

    Thomas Jefferson, *Notes on the State of Virginia* (Gloucester, Mass.: Peter
    Smith, 1976), p. 155.

## Chapter 6. The Limits of Private Solutions to Public Problems

1. David Popenoe, *Disturbing the Nest: Family Change and Decline in Modern
   Societies* (New York: Aldine de Gruyter, 1988), p. 78.

2. See, for example, Vonnie C. McLoyd, "The Impact of Economic Hardship
   on Black Families and Children: Psychological Distress, Parenting, and
   Socioeconomic Development," *Child Development* 61 (1990): 311–46;
   Cheryl D. Hayes, John L. Palmer, and Martha J. Zaslow, eds., *Who Cares for
   America's Children? Child Care Policy for the 1990s* (Washington, D.C.:
   National Academy Press, 1990), p. 57.

3. Burton L. White, *Educating the Infant and Toddler* (Lexington, Mass.: D.C. Heath, 1988), pp. 23–26.

4. Richard L. Zweigenhaft and G. William Domhoff, *Blacks in the White Establishment? A Study of Race and Class in America* (New Haven: Yale University Press, 1991), p. 160.

5. James H. S. Bossard, *The Sociology of Child Development* (New York: Harper & Brothers, 1948), p. 278.

6. Arlie Russell Hochschild, with Anne Machung, *The Second Shift* (New York: Viking, 1989).

7. Deborah L. Jacobs, "Back from the Mommy Track: No Matter How Short the Child-Care Detour, Many Women Pay a High Price to Return to the Corporate Road," *New York Times,* October 9, 1994, section 3, pp. 1, 6.

8. Marianne A. Ferber and Brigid O'Farrell with La Rue Allen, eds., *Work and Family: Policies for a Changing Work Force* (Washington, D.C.: National Academy Press, 1991), pp. 155–78.

9. Rosanna Hertz, *More Equal Than Others: Women and Men in Dual-Career Marriages* (Berkeley: University of California Press, 1986), pp. 147–95.

10. On group child care, see Alison Clarke-Stewart, *Daycare,* rev. ed. (Cambridge, Mass.: Harvard University Press, 1993); Martin O'Connell and Amara Bachu, "Who's Minding the Kids? Child Care Arrangements, Fall 1988." *Current Population Reports,* ser. P-70, no. 30 (Washington, D.C: U.S. Government Printing Office, 1992); Hayes, Palmer, and Zaslow, eds., *Who Cares for America's Children?*

11. Marcie Whitebook, Carollee Howes, and Deborah Phillips, *Who Cares? Child Care Teachers and the Quality of Care in America: Final Report of the National Child Care Staffing Study* (Oakland, Calif.: Child Care Employee Project, 1989).

# References

Alwin, Duane F. "Social Stratification, Conditions of Work, and Parental Social-ization Values." In *Social and Moral Values: Individual and Societal Perspectives,* edited by Nancy Eisenberg, Janusz Reykowski, and Ervin Staub, 327–46. Hillsdale, N.J.: Erlbaum, 1989.

Anderson, Lisa. "Who Keeps an Eye on the Nannies?" *Chicago Tribune,* May 29, 1988, section 5, pp. 2, 4.

Argyle, Michael. *The Psychology of Social Class.* New York: Routledge, 1994.

Ayres, B. Drummond, Jr. "California: Feinstein Attacking Opponent for Illegal Nanny." *New York Times,* October 30, 1994, p. A23.

Baumgartner, M. P. *The Moral Order of a Suburb.* New York: Oxford University Press, 1989.

Beck, Joan. *How to Raise a Brighter Child.* New York: Pocket Books, 1991.

Berg, Barbara J. *The Crisis of the Working Mother: Resolving the Conflict Between Family and Work.* New York: Summit Books, 1986.

Berger, Joseph. "The Story of a Nanny, From Care to Calamity." *New York Times,* April 18, 1993, p. 40.

Best, Joel. *Threatened Children: Rhetoric and Concern about Child Victims.* Chicago: University of Chicago Press, 1990.

Bossard, James H. S. *The Sociology of Child Development.* New York: Harper & Brothers, 1948.

Bourdieu, Pierre. *Distinction: A Social Critique of the Judgment of Taste.* Translated by R. Nice. Cambridge, Mass.: Harvard University Press, 1984.

———, and J. C. Passeron. *Reproduction in Education, Society, and Culture.* Beverly Hills, Calif.: Sage, 1977.

"Caught!" *New York Times* [Editorial]. October 30, 1994, Section 4, 14.

Clarke-Stewart, Alison. *Daycare.* Rev. ed. Cambridge, Mass.: Harvard University Press, 1993.

Coates, James. "Young Mormon Women Much in Demand as Nannies." *Arizona Daily Star,* March 1, 1987, section E, p. 11.

Colen, Shellee. "'Just a Little Respect': West Indian Domestic Workers in New York City." In *Muchachas No More: Household Workers in Latin America and the Caribbean,* edited by Elsa M. Chaney and Mary Garcia Castro, 171–94. Philadelphia: Temple University Press, 1989.

Collins, Randall. *The Credential Society.* New York: Academic Press, 1979.

Colvin, Richard Lee. "Taping a Gut Instinct." *Los Angeles Times,* September 26, 1991, pp. B1, B8.

Davis, Don. *The Nanny Murder Trial.* New York: St. Martin's Paperbacks, 1993.

Dill, Bonnie Thornton. "Across the Boundaries of Race and Class: An Exploration of the Relationship Between Work and Family Among Black Female Domestic Servants." Ph.D. diss., New York University, 1979.

Downs, Anthony. "The Controversial Aspect of the Atlanta Region's Future." *Brookings Review* (Summer 1994): 27–31.

Dreskin, Wendy, and William Dreskin. *The Day Care Decision: What's Best for Your Child.* New York: M. Evans., 1983.

Edgeworth, Maria, and Richard Lovell Edgeworth. *Practical Education.* Boston: Samuel Parker, 1823.

Ehrenreich, Barbara. *Fear of Falling: The Inner Life of the Middle Class.* New York: Harper Perennial, 1989.

Elkind, David. *The Hurried Child.* Reading, Mass.: Addison-Wesley, 1981.

Fairchilds, Cissie. *Domestic Enemies: Servants and Their Masters in Old Regime France.* Baltimore: Johns Hopkins University Press, 1984.

Fallows, Deborah. *A Mother's Work.* Boston: Houghton Mifflin, 1985.

Ferber, Marianne A., and Brigid O'Farrell, with La Rue Allen, eds. *Work and Family: Policies for a Changing Work Force.* Washington, D.C.: National Academy Press, 1991.

Foner, Nancy. "The Jamaicans: Race and Ethnicity Among Migrants in New York City." In *New Immigrants in New York,* edited by Nancy Foner, 195–217. New York: Columbia University Press, 1987.

Fraser, Ronald. *In Search of a Past: The Manor House, Annersfield, 1933–1945.* London: Verso, 1984.

Gardner, Ralph, Jr. "The Preschool Grovel." *New York Observer,* July 4–11, 1994, p. 13.

Gathorne-Hardy, Jonathan. *The Rise and Fall of the British Nanny.* London: Hodder and Stoughton, 1972.

Glenn, Evelyn Nakano. *Issei, Nisei, War Bride: Three Generations of Japanese American Women in Domestic Service.* Philadelphia: Temple University Press, 1986.

———. "Racial Ethnic Women's Labor: The Intersection of Race, Gender, and Class Oppression." In *Gender, Family, and Economy: The Triple Overlap,* edited by Rae Lesser Blumberg, 173–201. Newbury Park, Calif.: Sage, 1991.

Gugliotta, Guy. "The Central American Exodus: Grist for the Migrant Mill." In *The Caribbean Exodus,* edited by Barry B. Levine, 171–82. New York: Praeger, 1987.

Harper, Lucinda. "Many Flout Law on Reporting Taxes for Domestic Help: Some Receive Rude Surprises; Complexity and Expense Discourage Compliance." *Wall Street Journal,* April 15, 1992, p. 1.

Hayes, Cheryl D., John L. Palmer, and Martha J. Zaslow, eds. *Who Cares for America's Children? Child Care Policy for the 1990s.* Washington, D.C.: National Academy Press, 1990.

Heath, Shirley Brice. *Ways with Words: Language, Life, and Work in Communities and Classrooms.* Cambridge: Cambridge University Press, 1983.

Heer, David M. *Undocumented Mexicans in the United States.* American Sociological Association Rose Monograph Series. Cambridge: Cambridge University Press, 1990.

Hernandez, Raymond. "Baby Sitter Charged with Shaking Baby to Death." *New York Times,* May 5, 1993, p. B2.

Hertz, Rosanna. *More Equal than Others: Women and Men in Dual-Career Marriages.* Berkeley: University of California Press, 1986.

Heyns, Barbara. *Summer Learning and the Effects of Schooling.* New York: Academic Press, 1978.

Hochschild, Arlie, with Anne Machung. *The Second Shift: Working Parents and the Revolution at Home.* New York: Viking, 1989.

Holloway, Susan D., and Bruce Fuller. "The Great Child-Care Experiment: What Are the Lessons for School Improvement?" *Educational Researcher* 21 (1992): 12–19.

Horn, Pamela. *The Rise and Fall of the Victorian Servant.* New York: St. Martin's Press, 1975.

Jacobs, Deborah L. "Back from the Mommy Track: No Matter How Short the Detour, Many Women Pay a High Price to Return to the Corporate Road." *New York Times,* October 9, 1994, section 3, pp. 1, 6.

Jefferson, Thomas. *Notes on the State of Virginia.* Gloucester, Mass.: Peter Smith, 1976.

Joffe, Carole E. *Friendly Intruders: Childcare Professionals and Family Life.* Berkeley: University of California Press, 1977.

Kemble, Frances Anne. *Journal of a Residence on a Georgia Plantation in 1838–1839.* New York: Knopf, 1984.

Kleinfeld, N. R. "An Open Door to Disaster: Darker Side of Nanny Business: Children's Lives at Risk." *New York Times,* December 9, 1991, pp. B1, 4.

Kohn, Melvin L. *Class and Conformity: A Study in Values.* 2nd ed. Chicago: University of Chicago Press, 1977.

———, Atsushi Naoi, Carrie Schoenbach, Carmi Schooler, and Kazimierz Slomczynski. "Position in the Class Structure and Psychological Functioning in the United States, Japan, and Poland." *American Journal of Sociology* 95 (1990): 964–1008.

Lareau, Annette. *Home Advantage: Social Class and Parental Intervention in Elementary Education.* London: Falmer Press, 1989.

Leach, Penelope. *Children First: What Our Society Must Do—And Is Not Doing— for Our Children Today.* New York: Knopf, 1994.

LeVine, Robert A. "Women's Schooling, Patterns of Fertility, and Child Survival." *Educational Researcher* 16 (1987): 21–27.

Lipman, Joanne. "The Nanny Trap." *Wall Street Journal,* April 14, 1993, p. 1.

Lorence, B. W. "Parents and Children in Eighteenth Century Europe." *History of Childhood Quarterly: Journal of Psychohistory* 1 (1974): 1–30.

Lubeck, Sally. *Sandbox Society: Early Education in Black and White America.* London: Falmer Press, 1985.

Manning, Anita. "Nutty Nannies: Parents' Worst Nightmare." *USA Today,* January 13, 1992, pp. 1D, 2D.

McCarthy, Kevin F., and R. Burciaga Valdez. *Current and Future Effects of Mexican Immigration in California.* Santa Monica, Calif. Rand Corporation, May 1986.

McCartney, Kathleen, and Elizabeth Jordan. "Parallels Between Research on

Child Care and Research on School Effects." *Educational Researcher* 19 (1990): 21–27.

McLoyd, Vonnie C. "The Impact of Economic Hardship on Black Families and Children: Psychological Distress, Parenting, and Socioeconomic Development." *Child Development* 61 (1990): 311–46.

"The Nanny Tax, Improved." *New York Times,* October 7, 1994, p. A30.

Nelson, Margaret K. *Negotiated Care: The Experience of Family Day Care Providers.* Philadelphia: Temple University Press, 1990.

Newman, Katherine S. *Falling from Grace: The Experience of Downward Mobility in the American Middle Class.* New York: Vintage, 1988.

Palmer, Phyllis. *Domesticity and Dirt: Housewives and Domestic Servants in the United States, 1920–1945.* Philadelphia: Temple University Press, 1989.

"Parents of Dead Child Say They Suspected Abuse by Nanny." *New York Times,* November 10, 1993, p. B8.

Perlmann, Joel. *Ethnic Differences: Schooling and Social Structure Among the Irish, Italians, Jews & Blacks in an American City, 1880–1935.* Cambridge: Cambridge University Press, 1988.

Peterson, M. Jeanne. "The Victorian Governess: Status Incongruence in Family and Society." In *Suffer and Be Still: Women in the Victorian Age,* edited by Martha Vicunis, 3–19. Bloomington: Indiana University Press, 1973.

Popenoe, David. *Disturbing the Nest: Family Change and Decline in Modern Societies.* New York: Aldine de Gruyter, 1988.

Portes, Alejandro, and Ruben G. Rumbaut. *Immigrant America: A Portrait.* Berkeley: University of California Press, 1990.

Presser, Harriet B. "Employment Schedules Among Dual-Earner Spouses and the Division of Household Labor by Gender." *American Sociological Review* 59 (1994): 348–64.

Priestley, Joseph. *Miscellaneous Observations Relating to Education, More Especially as It Respects the Conduct of the Mind.* Millwood, N.Y.: Kraus Reprint Company, 1977 [1796].

Rollins, Judith. *Between Women: Domestics and Their Employers.* Philadelphia: Temple University Press, 1985.

Romero, Mary. *Maid in the U.S.A.* New York: Routledge, 1992.

Rosenbaum, David E. "Usually, the Illegality in Domestic Work is Benefits Denied." *New York Times,* January 31, 1993, section 4, p. 5.

Scarr, Sandra. *Mother Care/Other Care.* New York: Basic Books, 1984.

Senior, Jennifer. "In Washington, Au Pairs Are Bipartisan Choice for Child Care." *New York Times,* April 21, 1994, p. C9.

Shavit, Yossi, and Hans-Peter Blossfeld, eds. *Persistent Inequality: Changing Educational Attainment in Thirteen Countries.* Boulder, Colo.: Westview Press, 1993.

Singer, Elly. *Child-Care and the Psychology of Development.* London: Routledge, 1992.

South, Scott J., and Glenna Spitze. "Housework in Marital and Nonmarital Households." *American Sociological Review* 59 (1994): 327–47.

Stipek, Deborah, Sharon Milburn, Darlene Clements, and Denise H. Daniels. "Parents' Beliefs About Appropriate Education for Young Children." *Journal of Applied Developmental Psychology* 13 (1992): 293–310.

Timnick, Lois, and John H. Lee. "Three Children Killed When Flames Engulf Pacific Palisades Home." *Los Angeles Times,* March 21, 1989, section 1, p. 3.

Tobin, Joseph J., David Y. H. Wu, and Dana H. Davidson. *Preschool in Three Cultures: Japan, China, and the United States.* New Haven, Conn.: Yale University Press, 1989.

Trumbach, Randolph. *The Rise of the Egalitarian Family: Aristocratic Kinship and Domestic Relations in Eighteenth-Century England.* London: Academic Press, 1978.

Tucker, Susan. *Telling Memories Among Southern Women: Domestic Workers and Their Employers in the Segregated South.* Baton Rouge: Louisiana State University Press, 1988.

White, Burton L. *Educating the Infant and Toddler.* Lexington, Mass.: D. C. Heath, 1988.

———. *The First Three Years of Life.* 2nd ed. New York: Simon & Schuster, 1993.

Whitebook, Marcie L., Carollee Howes, and Deborah Phillips. *Who Cares? Child Care Teachers and the Quality of Care in America.* Final Report. National Child Care Staffing Study. Oakland, Calif.: Child Care Employee Project, 1989.

Wilkinson, Tracy. "Fatal Fire: Neighbors Can Only Shake Heads." *Los Angeles Times,* March 22, 1989, section 2, p. 1.

Williams, Patricia J. *The Alchemy of Race and Rights: Diary of a Law Professor.* Cambridge, Mass.: Harvard University Press, 1991.

Winnick, Louis. *New People in Old Neighborhoods: The Role of New Immigrants in Rejuvenating New York's Communities.* New York: Russell Sage Foundation, 1990.

Wrigley, Julia. "Do Young Children Need Intellectual Stimulation? Experts' Advice to Parents, 1900–1985." *History of Education Quarterly* 29 (1989): 41–75.

———. "Servants and Cultural Transmission Within English Families." Paper presented at the annual meeting of the American Sociological Association, San Francisco, August 1989.

Zinsser, Caroline. *Raised in East Urban: Child Care Changes in a Working-Class Community.* New York: Teachers College Press, 1991.

Zweigenhaft, Richard L., and G. William Domhoff. *Blacks in the White Establishment? A Study of Race and Class in America.* New Haven: Yale University Press, 1991.

# *Index*

Accommodations: for au pairs, 51; for live-in caregivers, 37, 136, 138, 152*n*15
Addiction in families, 83
African-American caregivers: as caregivers, 10–11, 129; as domestic workers, 10; racial prejudice of employers against, 10
Agencies, *see* Au pair agencies; Domestic employment agencies
Age of child: attachment with caregiver related to, 40–41; parental approach to language issues related to, 41–42; type of nanny hired related to, 12
Alcoholism in families, 83
Allen, La Rue, 157*n*8
Alwin, Duane F., 149*n*9
Anderson, Lisa, 155*n*7
Anxiety of parents: boyfriends or husbands of caregivers and, 91; children's performance and, 14–15; language issues and, 39; possible accidents and, 39–40; reprisals in conflicts with caregivers and, 93–94; safety of children and, 114; theft and, 46, 91–92

Argyle, Michael, 156*n*12
Art classes, 126
Attachment between child and caregiver: class subordinate caregivers and, 36; servants in earlier periods and, 12–13
Au pair agencies, 51, 67–68, 69, 98
Au pairs, 3; availability of, 51–52; countries of origin of, 52; cultural exchange element of using, 67–68; expectations of parents regarding, 69–70; firing of, 98; housekeeping tasks performed by, 26, 63–64; perspective of, 63–65; social lives of, 70–71, 135; treatment of, as servant, 68–69
Authority: British nannies and, 72; caregivers' lack of, 35; Caribbean caregivers and, 106; class peer caregivers and, 43, 66; of fathers, 85–86; *see also* Control issues
Autonomy of children: emphasis of parents on, 15–16; reaction of caregivers to, 16